THE NEW DIET FOR LIFE

Gwyneth Dover appears regularly on television and has been featured on *TVam*, *Bazaar*, and the *Miriam Stoppard Show*. Her other best-selling book, *Sweets without Sinning*, is published by Sidgwick & Jackson. Gwyneth has also been featured on many radio programmes and has lectured on disease prevention, fitness and health alongside top heart surgeons, quite apart from giving cookery demonstrations all over Britain. In 1989 she was invited by the *Daily Telegraph* to act as dietary and health expert for their pre-retirement cruises and in 1991 was fitness, diet and health lecturer for the CTC Canary Cruise.

With her husband Richard she won the 'Here's to Health' award in 1987. They live in a farmhouse in North Yorkshire which they converted themselves.

D082773

GWYNETH DOVER

The New
DIET
FOR
LIFE

PAN BOOKS
LONDON, SYDNEY AND AUCKLAND

First published as *A Diet for Life* 1989
by Sidgwick & Jackson Limited.
This revised edition published 1992 by
Pan Books Ltd, Cavaye Place, London SW10 9PG
in association with Sidgwick & Jackson Limited

1 3 5 7 9 8 6 4 2

© Gwyneth Dover 1992

The right of Gwyneth Dover to be identified
as author of this work has been asserted
by her in accordance with the Copyright,
Designs and Patents Act 1988.

ISBN 0 330 32255 9

Photoset by Parker Typesetting Service, Leicester

Printed in England by Clays Limited, St Ives plc

I would like to dedicate this book to my husband, Richard, and to my mum and dad who have had to tolerate my 'ups' and 'downs' while writing it. Without the love, support, encouragement and bullying of Richard I would never have put pen to paper and so I thank him from the bottom of my heart.

CONTENTS

WINNING CHANGES

RICHARD and I were married on 31 August 1974. It was the happiest day of my life. The picture people saw was one of happiness, kindness, success and love. Yet there was another, bleak, side to this picture of which people were unaware.

Serious heart disease had plagued Richard, and all his family, for many years. Richard had a blood cholesterol level over four times the norm, his heart was enlarged, a valve leaked and he had advanced artherosclerosis which resulted in the crippling angina pains between his shoulder blades. By the time Richard was thirty-five he had already suffered three major heart attacks. He was lucky to be alive.

Our lifestyle at that time was what I would call 'normal'. We ate an 'ordinary' diet dominated by meat, processed foods and dairy products. And, although I had started to research the area of diet and health, I still placed my trust in the doctors and changed our diet only marginally. Our exercise was minimal. By 1976 Richard could hardly walk. His weight was falling rapidly. He was constantly tired. Our hopes for the future were looking increasingly bleak.

As Richard became progressively worse the answer from the medical profession was to increase the dosage of drugs. These were useless and the side effects terrible. It seemed as if the doctors were merely moving around the deckchairs on the *Titanic* instead of trying to save the ship. I did not intend to lose Richard – at least not without a fight. And fight we did.

I began to spend more and more time in medical libraries searching out any information that was available on diet and health. I found most information in obscure journals from the USA as they were the pioneers of this research. We scoured every health magazine and health book with the proverbial fine tooth comb for any relevant information. Information on this topic was, to say the least, sparse at that time. I was considered an out and out crank for my efforts.

As a result of my new-found knowledge I modified our lifestyle drastically. Richard stopped smoking – with a great struggle. Our diet was changed. No red meats, no processed food, no egg yolks, no salt, no high-fat dairy products. We switched to white meat, fish, skimmed milk, cottage cheese, polyunsaturated margarine, fibre and lecithin. (Lecithin, which helps reduce blood cholesterol levels, occurs in many foods in small amounts, but to have enough, we add lecithin granules to our breakfast cereals.) Exercise was difficult as Richard was too ill to manage anything energetic.

The sad thing was that these changes seemed to be too little too late. Richard was still getting worse. By 1977 he was so ill that he spent much of the time in bed. Even the most basic movements caused him pain. He couldn't even peel and eat an orange without experiencing severe pain.

Richard's brother had similar, although less severe, heart problems and had a coronary bypass operation. It was arranged, with some difficulty, for Richard to see the same consultant. After investigations we were told that the news was good and bad. Richard was dangerously ill but operable.

We waited patiently for the operation date. The normal waiting time of three months passed without word of a date. Six months dragged by and still nothing. I rang the consultant on many occasions asking for an operation date, explaining that Richard was getting weaker by the day. After much pestering and persuasion we were given a date: 13 March 1978. We had waited eleven months. I consoled myself with the thought that Richard could not be as urgent a case as I thought, otherwise they would have operated much earlier. I could not have been further from the truth.

Richard had been placed on a 'cold' list. He was expected to die before the operation date and, even had he had the operation without a long wait, was expected to die on the operating table. He had an 80 per cent chance of dying during the operation. The consultants could not explain how he had survived for so long. He should have been dead. One consultant called it 'a miracle'. So maybe the changes we had made in our lifestyle had had more of an effect than I thought.

Richard did survive the operation and surprised everyone by making a quick and full recovery. The doctors were amazed. This was Richard's last chance and we were going to make the most of it. Together we decided that having status, money and success was not much use if you were dead, so Richard gave up his career in the rat race. My research had led us down the path of a vegetarian-type diet with no saturated fats and cholesterol. Everything was, and is, home-made to ensure that it is us, and not the manufacturers, who control what we eat.

We tried to persuade the doctors to take Richard off the 'cholesterol controlling' drugs, that were useless anyway, and to try our way – diet. After much argument they reluctantly agreed. Within four weeks Richard's cholesterol level was down to normal. The medical profession was amazed. Richard was carefully monitored for a year. He was then discharged – with a normal cholesterol level!

Today people don't believe that Richard has heart disease. He has the energy and stamina of a twenty-year-old. Looking at Richard now, even I find it incredibly difficult to imagine how very ill and near to death he was. Yet, at the same time, the memories of that period are so very vivid in my mind.

In 1982 we bought a derelict barn in the Yorkshire Dales and converted it – ourselves. The only thing we did not do was the plastering. We tried but just could not get the hang of it at all – there was more plaster on us than the walls. In fact, Richard bought me a lovely present for one of our wedding anniversaries – a cement mixer. He's very romantic! The two acres of 'jungle' are being landscaped and an organic vegetable plot cultivated and looked after by Richard. He is one of the most energetic people I know. Someone once said to Richard that he was 'the greatest comeback since Lazarus' and it's true.

In 1987 Richard and I became the very first winners of the Here's to Health Award. *Here's Health* magazine was searching for the healthiest couple in the UK. We entered the competition and won. That award changed my life for it made me realize that people were still crying out for information on healthy eating. I left my career as a polytechnic lecturer in financial economics and decided to write a book on healthy eating instead.

In 1987 we opened up our home as a country house, specializing in healthy cuisine. We tried gently to persuade people to eat a healthier breakfast than the 'normal' high-fat 'fry-up'. The healthy vegetarian breakfasts became far more popular than the traditional with our guests. We gained quite a reputation for them. Some people will never change, but we have managed to open the eyes of many who have stayed with us.

Richard, I am glad to say, is as fit as a lop (flea, to those who don't know Yorkshire terms). He is not on any medication. He never has to see a doctor. He is healthy, fit and happy. In fact we have just completed yet another conversion project. We have transformed some shepherds' cottages into three *en suite* bedrooms. What a mammoth task that was – certainly not for anyone lacking in energy! That says everything, doesn't it? The picture is no longer tainted by a bleak side. We now have a happy and healthy future to look forward to.

I decided to write this book in an effort to make people aware of the hidden dangers lurking in our traditional diet. The information contained in my book is based on over eighteen years of research. I know the problems and pitfalls of changing your diet – I've lived through them all. With luck, you can learn by my mistakes and experiences.

Richard and I both sincerely hope that our story will give courage to people in similar situations and inspire others to change their diet. The pain and suffering we went through can be avoided so very easily. The major diseases are preventable, and treatable, by eating a healthier diet. Don't wait until you are in the position that Richard and I were in.

CHAPTER ONE

IS YOUR DIET KILLING YOU?

IT MAY seem a silly question to some people, but I am quite serious when I ask the question: 'Is your diet killing you?' Most people see the western-style diet as being healthy. After all, people rarely die of starvation or suffer from malnutrition these days. And the days of widespread scurvy and rickets are gone. The majority of people enjoy more than adequate amounts of food and obtain all the necessary nutrients. Our average height and lifespan have increased – so too has our weight. The health problems associated with inadequate diet which were once rife are now relatively rare. So it would seem that all we have to do to remain healthy is carry on eating and drinking in the old way. There is no problem with the western diet. Or is there?

It is quite true that the health problems associated with poor nutrition, such as deficiency diseases, have declined rapidly in the West. As our income levels have increased the pattern of our consumption of food and drink has changed. The problem of the western diet is not under-nutrition but over-nutrition. This has led to people becoming increasingly unhealthy. Diseases such as cancer, strokes, high blood pressure and heart attacks are all too common in our society. And, what's more, we seem to accept these diseases as being inevitable. We abdicate our responsibilities, sit back and wait for these diseases to affect us and our families.

All we have to do to illustrate the point is to look at the major health problems that dominate our society today.

Heart disease is the number one killer in many western countries. In fact the UK has the dubious honour of being top of the world league table for deaths caused by heart disease. Cancer, the disease that most people fear more than any other, has increased rapidly in the western world. Other diseases, including strokes, gallstones, piles, constipation, diabetes, high blood pressure, gout and other forms of arthritis, have all shown enormous increases.

These diseases are 'diseases of affluence' and have been increasingly linked to our diet. Many of our common diseases are virtually unknown in less affluent societies where the diet is low in fat, low in salt and high in fibre. Yet, when these same societies become more affluent – or westernized – their eating patterns change and the diseases of affluence begin to appear. In fact, when people from a country where the diseases of affluence are rare emigrate to a country where they are common, certain interesting changes in health patterns occur. The immigrants, too, become candidates for heart disease, cancer, strokes, high blood pressure and so on. So clearly it is not that certain populations have an inherited immunity to these diseases. The major change that has taken place in the lives of these people is their diet. It is the change to a diet high in fat, sugar and salt and low in fibre that is thought to be the major cause of these 'new' health problems.

The major differences between our diet today and that of less affluent countries – not to mention our diet in the past – is striking. For one thing the meat consumed in less affluent countries is of a totally different type because it usually comes from wild or domestically reared animals, and rarely from those that have been intensively reared. As a result the meat's fat content is very much lower because the animals have been far more active and have not been pumped full of hormones. The fat is also of the healthier polyunsaturated type rather than the highly unhealthy saturated fat that intensively produced meat contains.

Vegetables play a much more prominent role in the diet of less affluent societies than in the affluent West. Vegetables are used as the basis for most meals and are not thought of as being a mere accompaniment to meat. The prominence of vegetables is important because they provide people not only with valuable nutrients but also with fibre.

People in the West also obtain quite a lot of their fat from dairy products while in less affluent countries dairy products play a minor role in the diet.

Many research programmes have been concerned with the links between cancer and diet. In 1981 the eminent scientist Richard Doll, world renowned for his research on cancer, published a report which collated all available evidence regarding human cancer and identifiable causes. The findings were that 35 per cent of all deaths from cancer were caused by diet. Tobacco came next, accounting for 30 per cent. Diet was singled out as the most important causative factor in cancer formation. Yet although we hear with almost monotonous regularity about the risks of smoking, we hear little of the risks associated with diet. Don't get me wrong. I am totally against smoking and support all anti-smoking campaigns. What I find increasingly difficult to accept is the lack of awareness about the hazards of a bad diet. And it is not that the case has not been proved. It has.

The most recent link between diet and cancer appears to be concerned with breast cancer. This is the number one killer of women and is probably feared more than any other form of cancer. Once again the culprit is thought to be saturated fat. Women who consume saturated fat, in the form of red meats and dairy products, on a regular daily basis are more at risk from breast cancer than women who are either vegetarians or vegans or who eat only white meat and fish. The link between breast cancer and saturated fat intake has been found in many studies undertaken in various countries.

Changes in our diet should reduce the risk of cancer and research has in fact shown this to be true. The common denominator in the research programmes is fat. As the consumption of fat in the form of meat and dairy products increases, so the number of deaths from cancer rises. The correlation is too strong to ignore.

The evidence pointing to diet as the main causal factor of cancer is overwhelming and beyond doubt. The level of fat consumption and death rates from cancer move in unison. And as the research continues, the links between diet and cancer become increasingly strong. The time to act upon this information has arrived.

The link between heart disease and diet is another area which has been extensively researched in an international context. Once again the results confirm that countries with high animal-fat intake also have high death rates from coronary heart disease. Conversely, in countries where plant food predominates in the diet the mortality rate from heart disease is lower.

In 1947 an international research programme started which was to form the basis for continued research into diet and heart disease. The countries involved included the USA, Finland, the Netherlands, Italy, Yugoslavia, Germany and Japan. Nearly 13,000 men aged between 40 and 59 were monitored for coronary heart disease. This study found that deaths due to heart disease were strongly linked with high saturated-fat intake. Some countries, notably the USA and Australia, began to act on these findings. Their consumption of saturated fats began to fall quite dramatically, with people consuming less red meat and dairy products. Other countries, including the UK, ignored the information. Consequently, in countries such as Australia, the USA, Finland, Belgium, New Zealand and Japan, there was a reduction in the number of deaths from heart disease, while the UK rocketed to the top of the heart disease death league. The contrasts could not be more striking. Men aged 35–74 in England and Wales have a 200 per cent greater chance of dying from coronary heart disease than their Italian counterparts, 300 per cent greater than their French counterparts and a staggering 800 per cent greater than their opposite numbers in Japan.

The UK had a fairly healthy diet during, and just after, the Second World War because foods were on ration. The population had a low-fat diet forced on them by circumstances. But scarcity soon disappeared and relatively cheap butter, meat, cheese, eggs and milk swamped the market. This led to a rapid increase in the number of people dying from coronary heart disease. In 1988 one Briton died every three minutes of each day and night from heart disease and it still kills three in ten of all men and two in ten of all women in Britain, and that's a shocking 175,793 people in the year. It's the same number of people – 480 – who would die if a jumbo jet crashed every day. Approximately 300,000 people suffer a heart attack each year and 320,000 consult their doctor with angina. The treatment of coronary heart disease is estimated to cost the NHS over £500 million per year. In stark contrast only £10 million is spent each year on its prevention. Not very cost-effective is it?

Eighteen years ago Finland had the highest rate of death from heart disease in the world. But then health education improved which led to changes in the pattern of food consumption. Less saturated fat, less salt, less sugar and more fibre were eaten. Deaths from heart disease began to fall. Finland now has one of the most rapidly falling rates of heart disease in the world. People have been made aware of the risk factors and have adapted their lifestyles to minimize those risks.

Diet, therefore, can help or hinder the chance of contracting heart disease. In 1974 cholesterol levels were checked in Japanese schoolchildren. They were found to have levels 12 milligrams lower than their peers in Princeton, USA. Since that time there has been a major change in the eating habits of the Japanese people. Their diet has become far more westernized as they consume increasing quantities of chips, beefburgers, meat and dairy produce. In 1984 Japanese schoolchildren were tested for cholesterol levels and this time the result was quite different. The Japanese had 10 milligrams more cholesterol than their Princeton counterparts.

Some people convince themselves that it cannot happen to them and that such research is far removed from their lives. I know that we did at one time too. But it does happen, and what makes you think that you are immune? Heart disease is not limited to the old. The Vietnam War brought that point home to the American population. Most of the young soldiers who were killed were found to have advanced artery blockage caused by cholesterol deposits, a situation which leads directly to heart attack. The soldiers were only eighteen and nineteen years of age. In the UK, many primary schoolchildren have been found to show early signs of heart disease. The problems are there and need to be dealt with as a matter of urgency.

We should not see these diseases as unavoidable and inevitable because they are not. Some societies have never experienced high blood pressure and yet we associate this very common complaint with old age in our society. Why? Each one of us will know of someone who has died from heart disease or cancer and yet we still go on accepting it as the natural order of things. I am of the very strong opinion that we can do something positive to avoid these life-threatening diseases. And it is up to you to do it because nobody else will take responsibility for your life.

Every single person, whether adult or child, male or female, is potentially at risk from their diet. Quite literally, your diet could be killing you and your family.

CHAPTER TWO

WHAT IS A HEALTHY DIET ANYWAY?

WE HAVE been told by various bodies, ranging from the government to the medical profession, to eat a healthier diet. This is easier said than done. Before we can make any changes in our eating patterns we need to know something about the foods we eat. Basically, we need to reduce the amount of fat, sugar and salt in our diets and increase our fibre consumption. We also need to make sure that we obtain all the necessary nutrients such as vitamins and minerals. That's what this chapter is all about.

FAT FACTS

There seems to be an awful lot of confusion about fats, which is not in the least surprising. Words such as 'poly-unsaturated', 'unhydrogenated', 'essential fatty acids' (EFAs) and 'mono-unsaturated' are bandied about glibly but seldom adequately explained. Some famous-name margarines boast that they are 'high in polyunsaturates' but never tell us why this should be good for our health. We merely see healthy looking, attractive people in the advertisements and the link between health and their product is forged.

I firmly believe that we have to understand why certain foods are good, or bad, for us in order to make the necessary changes to our diet. Most of the time we are merely told that something is either good or bad and that's it. We are not given enough information to make informed choices about the foods we consume – and this is especially true about fats.

Contrary to popular opinion not all fats are bad for our health. Indeed, some fats are essential to us. But what types of fat you consume and in what quantities makes all the difference to whether it is beneficial or harmful.

Fat gives the highest energy of all nutrients. The term 'fat' not only describes butters, margarines, oils and the visible fat on meat, but also the invisible fats that most foods contain. Try lighting a peanut or a walnut – they burn like candles. The reason is that they contain over 50 per cent fat. The avocado pear is over 80 per cent fat, and so is the coconut. We can expect lean roast beef to contain 11 per cent of its weight in invisible fat. It really is astonishing how much fat our foods contain. However, there are some foods that are fat-free and these include fruits, most vegetables, egg white, sugar (though this of course is bad for you in other ways) and most beverages. So it is not all gloom and doom.

In the UK our average intake of fats amounts to 45 per cent of our total calorie intake. This is too high for a healthy diet. Various dietary guidelines, including reports from the World Health Organization (WHO) and the National Advisory Committee on Nutritional Education (NACNE), recommend that no more than 30 per cent of our calories should come from fat. But even more important is the type of fat we consume. No more than 10 per cent should be in the form of saturated fat. The remaining 20 per cent should be split equally between polyunsaturated and mono-unsaturated fats, which would account therefore, for 10 per cent each. Put like this, it all sounds extremely complicated, but it needn't be if you eat the right types of food.

Since 1978 fat consumption in the UK has remained at

its high level, stubbornly refusing to drop. However, the type of fat consumed has changed and is continuing to do so. We are moving towards the healthier type of polyunsaturated fats and away from saturated. But there is still a long way to go.

Saturated fats are a storage type of fat and provide us with a long-term supply of energy. The energy we get from food is expressed in terms of calories and most of us eat more than enough calories to give us sufficient energy. Should you deplete your store of fat, your body will convert protein and carbohydrates from the food you eat into saturated fat. Therefore, the consumption of saturated fats is unnecessary because our bodies can manufacture their own from other nutrients if required. Saturated fats also provide us with our 'padding' and most people feel that they have too much of this already. Saturated fats remain solid at room temperature and keep well.

There is nothing wrong with eating some saturated fat but this should not exceed 10 per cent of your total calorie intake. By eating more you are storing up ill health for your future and risk premature death. This is no idle threat – it is fact. Saturated fat increases the level of cholesterol in the blood by encouraging the liver to make more. The cholesterol is released into the bloodstream and then forms fatty deposits on the artery walls, blocking them up and restricting blood flow. Saturated fat also makes the blood much thicker and therefore increasingly prone to clotting. Heart disease, strokes, high blood pressure, various forms of cancer including breast and stomach, gallstones, diabetes and acne are just some of the diseases which are attributed to high intakes of saturated fat.

Polyunsaturated fats are a structural type of fat and

have many crucial functions in our bodies. They are essential if the brain and nerves are to develop and grow properly. They are incorporated into every single cell in our bodies. And, by making blood less sticky and less likely to clot, they keep the artery walls clear, allowing blood to flow freely. These structural fats cannot be manufactured by the body and so must form part of our diet. This is not as easy as it sounds because the traditional western diet not only contains far too much fat but also mostly contains the wrong type.

Because the body cannot imitate these crucial polyunsaturated fats they are called 'essential fatty acids' (EFAs) and we require 10 grams of them each day. Unlike saturated fats, they remain liquid at room temperature. Particularly good sources are seed oils and fish. An interesting fact about fat emerged in the early post-war years when research found that Eskimos suffered ten times less coronary heart disease than Danes. Both populations had fatty diets, so what was the difference? While the Danish diet was rich in saturated fat, the Eskimo diet was rich in fat gained from oily fish. This fat is high in polyunsaturates but, unlike the fat in oils and margarines, it is rich in Omega 3 – three EFAs of which the two most important are EPA (eicosapentanoic) and DHA (decosahexanoic). The Eskimos' blood also had a high ratio of the 'good' type of cholesterol (high density lipoprotein or HDL) to the 'bad' type (low density lipoprotein or LDL) and was far less likely to clot. Eskimos are protected from heart disease, strokes and cancer by their high intake of EFAs from oily fish, mackerel, sardines and seals, in spite of the fact that these foods are also high in saturated fat and cholesterol.

EFAs have been used extensively in the management of certain diseases. High blood cholesterol levels, for example, have been successfully treated with EFAs, which usually increase the 'good' type (HDL) and reduce the 'bad' type (LDL) of cholesterol in the blood. Other conditions that have responded well to EFA treatment are eczema, premenstrual tension (PMT), cardiovascular disease and high blood pressure. As the human body cannot manufacture EFAs, deficiency symptoms can arise if our diet is not supplying adequate amounts. These symptoms can range from dry skin to a failure to reproduce, and include increased water loss, metabolic disorders, weight loss and growth problems.

Did you know that if you use polyunsaturated fats in frying, some of the polyunsaturated fats become saturated when hot? In fact, the polyunsaturates will decline by between 10 per cent and 20 per cent over a short frying period. Any oil that is overheated and 'smokes' must never be reused and any oil that starts to foam is toxic and must not be used. If you must fry, use a mono-unsaturated oil as this remains stable when heated.

Mono-unsaturated fats are relatively new to our body of knowledge. They are usually described as 'neutral' because they seem to have no effect on our artery walls or on blood cholesterol levels. However, recent research suggests that they may act in a way similar to polyunsaturated fats. The main sources are olive oil and the fat found in poultry. In a recipe that requires some frying always use olive oil, or else a dry-fryer frying pan that needs hardly any oil at all, which has got to be good news, hasn't it?

Just when you thought it was safe to go out and buy a margarine with a label boasting 'high in polyunsaturates', there is another complication. Most margarines that use polyunsaturated fats would be liquid at room temperature. But this is not what the consumer wants. We want to be able to spread it on to our bread and rub it into flour to make pastry. It has to be practical. This difficulty is overcome by a manufacturing process known as hydrogenation. What happens is that hydrogen is added to any unsaturated fatty acids present in the oil. This changes the melting point of the oil, giving it a harder texture at room temperature. In effect this makes it saturated and very unhealthy. So next time you buy a tub of margarine read the label carefully, and if it has hydrogenated vegetable oils, or hydrogenated unsaturated fat, on the list of ingredients, don't buy it. It means that, although the fat is of vegetable origin and probably starts out being polyunsaturated, it has become saturated. It will have, therefore, the same effect on your body as animal fats. At the time of writing you can buy unhydrogenated margarine only from healthfood shops and not, unfortunately, from supermarkets. Fingers crossed that this situation may change in the near future.

And what about those low-fat spreads that are becoming increasingly popular? They are attractive both because they are lower in fat and because they have fewer calories than their traditional counterparts. These spreads contain only 40 per cent fat while, by law, butter and margarine have to contain a minimum of 80 per cent fat. In terms of calories, the spreads contain a little over half the amount in butter and margarine. However, we must remember that it is the type of fat that is important, not just the amount. So although we should make an effort to reduce the total amount of fats eaten, we should substitute polyunsaturated for saturated fats. Again, read the label carefully and choose a spread that is high in polyunsaturates.

It's relatively easy and painless both to reduce the total amount of fat you consume and to change the type of fat to polyunsaturated. Once you are familiar with the terminology you can replace the high saturated fat foods with a healthier alternative. It will become second nature once you get the hang of it.

THE FATS OF LIFE		
FOOD	HIGH FAT	LOW FAT
MEAT	beef, pork, mutton, lamb, bacon, sausages, meat pies, liver pâtés, duck, goose, processed meats	chicken (no skin), turkey, rabbit, pigeon, venison, pheasant
FISH	fried whitebait, fried scampi, taramasalata, canned salmon, fried cod in batter, fish fingers	all poached or steamed white fish
DAIRY PRODUCTS	butter, cream, cheddar cheese, other hard yellow cheeses, stilton, cheshire, cream cheese, parmesan, cheese spreads, full-fat milks, egg yolk	cottage cheese, low-fat soft cheese, half-fat hard cheese, fromage frais, low-fat spread, low-fat yogurt, skimmed milk, egg white
VEGETABLES, NUTS	crisps, low-fat crisps, frozen dried chips, avocado pears, nuts, nut butters	all potatoes cooked without fat, all vegetables, salads, peas, beans, lentils with no added fat

THE FIBRE FACTOR

Until fairly recently fibre, or roughage as it used to be called, was not a topic for polite conversation. In fact, fibre was rarely mentioned at all, let alone in company. Then in 1983 came the F-Plan diet which changed the whole concept of fibre. Suddenly what was a taboo subject became the topic of conversation in the most respectable places. Fibre gave endless material to top comedians all over the world. Fibre was now fashionable and not only respectable but funny as well. People began to talk about it in everyday conversations.

Despite all this new-found interest and publicity many people remain confused about fibre. 'What is fibre anyway?' 'What does it do?' 'Is it important?' 'How much do I need?' 'Where does fibre come from?' All are important questions which need answering if we are to understand the importance of fibre to our health.

The Committee on Medical Aspects of Food Policy (COMA) Report published in 1981 by the DHSS stated that 'an increase in the cereal fibre content of the diet would be beneficial'. This was reiterated in the findings of the NACNE Report, published in 1983, which stated that our 'fibre intake should be increased by 33 per cent to 30 grams per day. The increase should come from the consumption of more wholegrain cereal, fresh fruit and vegetables.' The NACNE Report stressed that these recommendations were not for people who were particularly 'at risk' but for the whole population. We are all at risk from the typical British diet.

Our consumption of fibre has been falling steadily throughout the twentieth century. We consume less cereal, especially oats and bread, than we used to and eat fewer potatoes. In fact, since the Second World War our consumption of bread and potatoes is down over 40 per cent. Moreover our consumption of fresh vegetables, especially the dark green high-fibre type, dropped by almost 20 per cent in the period 1978 to 1983. It is no wonder that over 40 per cent of us are constantly constipated and that over 25 per cent need to use commercial laxatives! One Area Health Authority in the UK instituted changes to the foods served in their hospitals by going over to high-fibre wholefoods. The result was spectacular, although predictable. They saved thousands of pounds in suppositories.

Fibre is what is left behind once our food has been digested and is turned into faeces. Dietary fibre hastens the passage of food through the intestine. And not only does fibre increase the bulk of faeces, it also ensures they are produced more frequently.

The importance of fibre in our diet has been under-estimated for many years. How many people have been brought up to believe that individuals will vary in the regularity of their bowel movements – from once a day to once a week? We have been led to believe that this is perfectly normal. We all have our own individual 'clock' tuned in to our particular needs. Sounds familiar? Well, this mode of thinking has been totally discredited now as research brings to light the crucial role of fibre in a healthy diet.

There are a number of different types of fibre and each one plays a specific role in our body. The fibre we obtain from wheat and wholegrain cereals, for example, absorbs water from the gut and this helps to increase the bulk of our faeces. This type of fibre is valuable in relieving constipation. Other types of fibre, from fruits, vegetables and beans, have been found to lower blood cholesterol levels by absorbing it and aiding its journey through the body. Some types of fibre are fermented by bacteria in the gut and the by-products of this process help to keep the large bowel healthy. The quicker the faeces pass through the body, the shorter the period that toxic sub-stances are in contact with the walls of the colon (the large bowel), so reducing the risk of cancer. It is, therefore, important to obtain our fibre from a wide variety of sources.

A lack of fibre in the diet has been linked to many major diseases with which we are all too familiar. Diseases such as heart disease, various cancers – particularly cancer of the bowel and breast – diabetes, diverticular disease, appendicitis, gall stones, obesity, tooth decay, varicose veins, haemorrhoids, hiatus hernia and constipation are thought to be preventable if fibre intake is increased. These diseases are not merely uncomfortable and a nuisance; they also kill. I am sure that every single person reading this will know of one person who is currently suffering from one of these diseases – and know of someone who has died prematurely. By eating increased amounts of fibre from a variety of goods many of these diseases could be prevented.

Dietary fibre is found in the leaves, roots, stems, seeds and fruits of plants. Nearly all vegetable foods contain some fibre. Foods made with wholewheat, containing the bran, are far richer sources of fibre than the refined milled types. If you eat wholemeal bread you are consuming 350 per cent more fibre than someone who eats white bread. A good bowl of wholewheat breakfast cereal will give you over sixteen times the fibre of its refined counterpart, such as cornflakes. Berries, such as blackberries and raspberries, contain higher levels of fibre than fleshy fruits such as apples, and dried fruits are excellent because the fibre is concentrated. Vegetables such as cabbage, peas and beans have the highest fibre levels relative to other vegetables.

So it needs only a few basic everyday changes to increase your fibre intake, without disrupting your diet too much by having to make radical changes. All you have to do is simply substitute unrefined foods for refined foods and eat plenty of fresh fruit, vegetables, beans and pulses. It is as easy as that.

SWEET TALK

There is no getting away from the fact that the western world generally, and the UK specifically, has a very sweet tooth. Sugar became a popular commodity in the UK around 1850 and consumption rose substantially until 1956. Average sugar consumption in 1855 was about 35 grams per person each day and this figure had risen to 140 grams by 1956. Since 1956, however, our sugar consumption has been falling steadily and stands at somewhere between 75 and 100 grams. This is still considered too high a level to be healthy.

According to the government's NACNE Report we should consume no more than 54 grams of sugar per day. This amounts to a maximum of ten teaspoons of sugar each day. At first this maximum may appear quite generous as we tend to think of sugar consumption as the spoonfuls we drop into our tea or coffee. But the picture is far more complicated than this. Sugar is used extensively in the manufacturing of most foods – and I don't just mean the obvious sweet-tasting foods like jam and cakes. About 60 per cent of our total intake of sugar is from manufactured or processed foods. So reducing your sugar intake is not as simple as merely halving the amount of sugar you take in your tea and coffee.

For the food manufacturer, sugar, once known as 'white gold', kills many birds with one stone. It tastes nice, it increases the shelf life of food products and adds a nice texture to the foods we eat. And, what's more, it is not only sweet foods that contain added sugar. Most savoury manufactured foods contain surprisingly high sugar levels. Tomato ketchup, for example, contains over 20 per cent sugar while sweet pickle has 30 per cent and chutney 50 per cent! That maximum of ten teaspoons of sugar a day starts to disappear rather quickly once we take into account the sugar added to foods by the manufacturers. A quick look at the table below highlights the problem well.

FOOD	AMOUNT	TEASPOONS OF SUGAR
Bran biscuit	1	3
Sparkling glucose drink	1 glass	7
Blackcurrant cordial	1 glass	6
Sugar-coated cereal	1 bowl	3½
Tinned fruit	1 small tin	5
Jelly	1 packet	19
Malted milk drink	3 tsp	2
Packet tomato soup	¼ packet	2
Baked beans	½ medium tin	2
Chocolate toffee bar	1	9

It is hardly surprising that most westerners obtain far too many of their calories from sugar. One glass of a sparkling glucose drink and a bran biscuit and that's it – you've reached the maximum limit.

In 1983 the Royal College of Physicians, in a report called 'Obesity', stated:

In Britain the consumption of sugar per head is higher than in most other countries and, apart from its effect on dental caries, sugar is an unnecessary source of energy in a community with such a widespread problem of obesity.

Clearly then the message is to reduce the total amount of sugar we consume. And that means the 'invisible' sugar contained in manufactured foods as well as the 'visible' sugar which we can control.

A major stumbling block in reducing our sugar consumption is that we find it very difficult to do so. Sugar is addictive and if you, like me, have been brought up on sweetened cordials and sweet sticky puddings, then you have a problem. Your taste buds will find water, unsweetened beverages and plainly cooked vegetables boring and unappetizing. However, perseverance will pay off. After a week without sugar you will begin to taste the natural flavour and sweetness in vegetables like carrots and parsnips. Your palate will feel cleaner and appreciate the fresh taste of food.

Not only this, your skin will begin to look smoother and your complexion clearer. Your eyes will be brighter and you will have lost a few pounds in the process. Kicking the sugar habit is the best thing you can do to enhance your natural beauty.

But why all this fuss and bother about sugar? What is wrong with it? The first problem with sugar is that it is devoid of nutrients. White sugar contains 99.5 per cent sucrose and no other nutrient. Demerara retains some of the colour and flavour of raw cane sugar but is little better than white in terms of nutrients. Other brown sugars are merely white sugar with added caramel, or some such syrup, to tint it brown! Calories obtained from sugar are, therefore, 'empty calories' as they provide nothing except calories.

Sugar also encourages us to over-eat and thus become fat. Our over-consumption of sugary, high-calorie foods is understandable because they do not fill our stomachs effectively. The satisfying feeling of being full soon disappears with such foods and within an hour we require more. It is a vicious circle which can be difficult to break.

We would be far better getting our calories from unrefined carbohydrate foods (such as brown rice, wholemeal bread and pasta), fruit and vegetables. In this way we would not only feel full for longer but also obtain essential nutrients.

Tooth decay is also caused by sugar, especially when it is eaten in a sticky form such as toffee. It is also thought to raise the amount of triglycerides (a form of fat) on the skin. The old wives' tale about not eating sugar if you have a greasy skin and spots has a lot of truth in it.

Serious diseases such as diabetes, heart disease and cancer have been linked to high sugar intake but this remains controversial. The research continues in its quest to find the answers. But the links between sugar and ill health have been made and we need to listen to and act upon all the current advice to reduce our consumption.

SHAKE OUT SALT

Salt is the main source of sodium in the diet. A 'normal' diet supplies about 12 grams of salt per day. The NACNE report recommends that this level is too high and should be reduced by approximately 50 per cent. Salt consumption should, therefore, be no more than 5 grams per day.

A high sodium diet is strongly associated with high blood pressure, strokes, heart attacks and stomach cancer. In fact every population in the world that has a high salt intake also has a problem with blood pressure. Conversely, those populations with low salt intakes have no blood pressure problems. So it is in our own interests to reduce our salt consumption.

As with sugar, salt is a cheap and valuable commodity

to the food manufacturers. It is used as a flavour enhancer and a preservative, so much of the salt we eat is in processed foods and hidden from us. We have little control over this salt addition, other than voting with our purchasing power and demanding salt-free foods. Table and cooking salt account for only about a quarter of all salt eaten in the UK. The remainder is in manufactured foods.

Most breakfast cereals contain added salt – and in quite high doses. Generally speaking, crisps and snack foods have relatively high salt levels. Almost all tinned vegetables have added salt as do tinned meats and tinned fish. And the humble stock cube can have as much as 40 per cent salt!

It has often been stated that sea salt is healthier than ordinary salt. However it is just as salty as ordinary salt and because it has larger grains you will tend to use more. So it is no better for your health.

It is better to give up salt gradually. Your taste buds will adapt to having less salt quite quickly and you will begin to appreciate the true flavours of food. If you tried to eliminate salt from your diet in one go you would probably find food so bland that you would give up the whole idea.

VITAL VITAMINS

Although most of us know something about vitamins, it's generally rather vague. Do you really know what vitamins do? How many there are? How much you need? Where you get them all from? Whether you need a supplement? Even the so-called 'experts' argue among themselves about vitamins, so what chance do the rest of us have!

There is, however, no argument about the fact that vitamins are essential to achieving good health. Vitamins are made by bacteria, plants or animals and are needed for growth and metabolism. Our bodies manufacture insufficient amounts and so our diet must supplement the supply.

Although the existence of vitamins was only discovered in 1912, people have been aware of their properties for centuries. The ancient Egyptians ate foods rich in vitamin A to cure night blindness – and that was 1,500 years before the birth of Christ. During the mid-eighteenth century sailors were given rations of lemon juice on their voyages to help combat the onset of scurvy. British seamen were called 'limeys' because of the lime juice rations they were given in the nineteenth century. But limes have a lower vitamin C content than lemons and outbreaks of scurvy reappeared.

Beriberi, rickets and pellagra were also common in the past but have been almost eliminated in the West now that most of us consume adequate amounts of vitamins. Minor vitamin deficiencies can lead to general feelings of malaise while major vitamin deficiencies can result in serious illness.

We need fifteen different vitamins, all of which perform different functions and are obtained from different foods. How much of these vitamins we need is a grey area. Most advanced countries give guidelines on the amounts required daily, usually called recommended daily amounts (RDAs), but these differ from country to country. Even within countries there is argument about the 'correct' levels needed. In Britain there are only RDAs for six of the vitamins. As research progresses and we find out more about the nature and role of vitamins the RDAs are amended accordingly. A few years ago the message was 'more means better', whereas the new message is rather more cautious. Research has shown that excessive doses of some vitamins can actually be harmful and, therefore, RDAs have been reassessed to take account of this new information. However, there is a growing demand for increasing RDAs in an attempt to prevent, or protect us from, diseases such as cancer and heart disease. The debate continues!

RDAs are merely averages and do not reflect the fact that people will require varying amounts of nutrients. After all, none of us is 'average'. RDAs should therefore be considered only as general guidelines and never as rigid figures. Many nutritionists argue that the UK need not bother about the quantity of vitamins consumed as our 'balanced' diet provides a more than adequate supply. However, research shows that much of the population is seriously short of many vitamins.

Vitamins are divided into water-soluble and fat-soluble groups. Vitamins A, D, E and K are fat soluble and stored in body fat or the liver. Because the body stores these vitamins, poisonous build-ups can develop. Excessive amounts should, therefore, be taken only under proper medical supervision. The water-soluble vitamins are B and C and excess amounts are normally excreted in the urine. However, vitamin B_{12} and folic acid can be stored in the liver but excess doses are not toxic. Fat-soluble vitamins are more stable in cooking and processing than water-soluble vitamins. This is because water-soluble vitamins leak out during cooking and many are destroyed by heat.

Vitamins are fragile and need to be handled in the right way if we are to retain their value. After all, we do not want to throw vitamins down the drain. So, how do we solve the case of the disappearing vitamins?

Buying Tips

Ensure that vegetables are fresh when you buy them. Root vegetables should feel firm and not spongy and leafy vegetables should be crisp and bright green.

Choose fresh fruit with a strong, bright colour. Fruit that seems heavy for its size is likely to be juicy and not dried out.

Buy smaller quantities of fruit and vegetables to eat on the day of purchase rather than stocking up for the week.

Use frozen fruit and vegetables if fresh are difficult to obtain, as they will contain more vitamins than fresh ones that have been stored for a long period.

Always buy fruit and vegetables when they are at their best and never when they are being sold off cheap because of age or bruising.

Buy unrefined, brown versions of pasta, rice, bread, flour and breakfast cereals.

Storage Tips

It is important to store vegetables in a cool, dark place. The fridge is ideal for small quantities.

Never store vegetables or fruit in polythene bags as they will sweat and lost vitamins.

Eat fresh fruit and vegetables as soon as possible.

Freezing your own fruit and vegetables is a good way to retain vitamins, but you must freeze them immediately after picking.

Preparation Tips

Peeling, grating, shredding and chopping expose surface to the air and allow vitamins to escape. Cut vegetables in larger chunks so less surface area is exposed. Cutting in 'thick sticks' rather than 'rounds' is a good idea for vegetables such as carrots, parsnips and courgettes.

VITAMIN	AVERAGE RDA	FUNCTIONS
A	750mc	Maintenance of healthy skin and hair. Necessary for colour and night vision Needed for growth, bones and teeth.
B_1 (Thiamin)	1.0mg	Essential for growth and life. Acts in converting glucose into energy in muscles and nerves. Assists the efficient transmission of messages to the brain.
B_2	1.5mg	Needed for growth in children. Maintenance of healthy skin and eyes, maintenance and repair of body tissues and mucous membranes. Releases energy from carbohydrates, fats and proteins.
B_3 (Nicotinic acid, niacin)	16.5mg	Maintains healthy skin, nerves, brain, tongue, digestive system.

DEFICIENCY SYMPTOMS	BEST VEGETARIAN SOURCES	OTHER SOURCES
Depression, rickets, bone softening and blindness.	Margarine, butter, egg yolks, yellow, orange and green vegetables, peaches, tomatoes, dried apricots, cheese, milk and cream.	Liver, eels, salmon, herring and mackerel.
Loss of appetite. Tiredness and emotional instability. Nausea. Lack of concentration, memory loss.	Brewer's yeast, yeast extract, brown rice, wheatgerm, nuts, pulses, soya flour, oats, wholemeal bread and wholegrain cereals.	Pork, liver, ham, bacon, heart, kidney, and cod's roe.
Sores on mouth corners, lips and greasy areas of skin. Skin and eye irritation. Inflamed tongue and lips. Hair loss.	Yeast extract, brewer's yeast, wheatgerm, dairy products, wheat bran, some breakfast cereals, soya flour, dark green vegetables, pulses, almonds, mushrooms and prunes.	All meats – especially liver, sardines, mackerel and roes.
Dermatitis, diarrhoea and dementia. Stress, depression, insomnia and irritability. Nausea and vomiting.	Yeast extract, brewer's yeast, wheat bran, nuts, soya flour, wholegrains, dairy products, wholemeal bread, dried fruit, brown rice, potatoes and pulses	Pig's liver, chicken, meat and fatty fish.

VITAMIN	AVERAGE RDA	FUNCTIONS
B_5 (Pantothenic acid)	4.7mg	Maintains healthy nerves and controls fat metabolism. Vital link in the chain releasing energy from food.
B_6 (Pyridoxine)	2.0mg	Essential for growth, blood formation, healthy skin and nerves. Protection against infection.
B_{12} (Cobalamin)	3.0mc	Maintains nervous system, builds genetic material (DNA) and helps in the formation of red blood cells. Needed for nerve insulation.
C	30mg	Essential for growing children. Important in maintaining health of bones, teeth, gums, cartilage, capillaries, connective tissue and in the use of folic acid and iron. Controls blood cholesterol levels, maintains healthy sex organs.

DEFICIENCY SYMPTOMS	BEST VEGETARIAN SOURCES	OTHER SOURCES
Headache, personality changes, extreme fatigue, pins and needles, stomach cramps and walking difficulties.	Brewer's yeast, yeast extract, nuts, wheatbran, wheatgerm, soya flour, eggs, wholegrains, pulses, mushrooms, vegetables and wholemeal bread.	Pig's liver, pig's kidney, poultry and meats.
Depression, headaches, skin disease, anaemia and premenstrual tension. Breast discomfort, swollen abdomen, kidney stones and artheriosclerosis.	Brewer's yeast, wheat bran, yeast extract, wheatgerm, oats, soya flour, bananas, nuts, brown rice, potatoes, vegetables, pulses, eggs and cheese.	Liver, kidney, meats and fatty fish.
Pernicious anaemia, nerve deterioration and confusion. Loss of co-ordination and memory. Menstrual disorders.	Eggs, cheese, milk, yogurt, yeast extract, breakfast cereals with added B_{12}, strong ale and comfrey leaves.	All animal foods.
Weakness, muscle and joint pain, irritability, bleeding gums, loose teeth, gingivitis and scurvy.	Brussel sprouts, citrus fruits, watercress, cabbage, all fruit and vegetables.	Liver and kidney.

VITAMIN	AVERAGE RDA	FUNCTIONS
D	10mc	Necessary for absorption of calcium from food and the hardening of bones and teeth.
E	10mg	Maintaining structure of cell membranes. Anti-blood clotting agent and blood vessel dilator. Maintains healthy blood vessels. Antioxidant. Increases 'safe' cholesterol. Protects vitamin A. Prevents artherosclerosis.
K	N/A	Control of blood clotting.
Folic acid	300mc	Needed in the formation of blood cells and production of genetic material (DNA and RNA). Necessary for growth, healthy nervous and digestive systems. Transmits hereditary characteristics. Anaemia. Birth defects at conception may be due to a deficiency; research continues.

DEFICIENCY SYMPTOMS	BEST VEGETARIAN SOURCES	OTHER SOURCES
Softening of the bones: rickets in children and osteomalacia in adults. Problems with joints.	Eggs, milk and margarine. Sunshine.	Fatty fish and cod liver oil.
Lack of vitality, apathy, irritability, lack of concentration, decreased sexual interest and muscle weakness.	Wheatgerm oil, soyabean oil, maize oil, safflower oil, sunflower oil and cod liver oil. Almonds and hazelnuts. Wholegrain breakfast cereals, wholemeal bread, dark green vegetables, eggs, margarine, cheese, tomatoes and pulses.	Shrimps, meat and fish.
Usually only newborn babies are deficient, which results in excess bleeding from the stomach and intestine.	Cauliflower, brussel sprouts, broccoli, lettuce, spinach, cabbage, tomatoes, string beans, potatoes and pulses.	Pig's liver, beef liver and meat.
Fatigue, breathlessness, irritability, insomnia and mental problems. Premature birth and habitual abortion. Can cause spina bifida in an unborn fetus.	Dark green vegetables, wheatgerm, brewer's yeast, nuts, wholemeal bread, wholegrain cereals, brown rice, citrus fruits, eggs and pulses.	

Prepare fruit and vegetables only just before use.

You will save vitamins if you wipe, rather than peel, the edible skins of fruits and vegetables.

Cut your vegetables with a sharp stainless-steel knife to avoid bruising.

Higher amounts of vitamins are contained in the dark green, outer leaves of green vegetables.

Cooking Tips

Eat vegetables raw as often as possible.

The best way to cook vegetables is either to steam or to microwave them.

Cook vegetables in the shortest possible time.

If you do need to boil vegetables use as little water as possible and always use the cooking liquor as part of the meal. This way you retain the vitamins that have 'leaked out' during cooking.

Always keep lids on saucepans otherwise vitamins escape with the steam.

Never add bicarbonate of soda to green vegetables during cooking – it may make them greener but it also robs them of vitamins.

Never soak fruit and vegetables in water.

The buying, preparation and cooking of foods are crucial in the fight to retain vitamins. However vitamins have yet another enemy waiting in the wings to destroy them – ourselves. Smoking destroys many vitamins as does alcohol. Stress also uses up vitamins. Other vitamin-destroyers include coffee, antibiotics, the contraceptive pill, aspirin and mineral oil laxatives.

MINERAL MATTERS

Until fairly recently minerals were completely over-shadowed by vitamins (pages 28–38). Now research has highlighted the important functions minerals perform in our bodies and brought to life an interest in them. But do we really understand minerals?

The first important point about minerals is that the body cannot manufacture them. If you do not get your supply from the foods you eat, then, quite simply, you do not get them. And it is important to get them if we are to lead full and healthy lives. Mineral deficiency can make you feel generally under the weather and ultimately lead to serious illness. So it is crucial to know how much of a mineral you require and what you get it from.

Nutritionally speaking, minerals are split into two groups: macro-elements and trace elements, depending on how much of a particular mineral we require. If we require a mineral in quantities in excess of 100 milligrams every day then it is classed as a macro-element. On the other hand, minerals that we require in smaller quantities, less than 100 milligrams every day, are in the trace element group. Neither group is more important than the other – they are both essential. Macro-elements are important in the transmission of nerve impulses, while trace elements are important in the formation of hormones and enzymes by the body.

As with vitamins, recommended daily amounts (RDAs) should be treated as a guide and not as a rigid figure to be adhered to at all costs. RDAs vary from country to country and change as new research comes to light. They are not unalterably carved in stone. And although we think of western countries as having generally good nutrition, some would say we have over-

RECOMMENDED DAILY AMOUNTS OF CALORIES AND PROTEIN

CHILDREN

AGE RANGE YEARS	SEX	CALORIES	PROTEIN grams
0–1	M	1200	30
	F	1100	27
1–2	M	1400	35
	F	1300	32
3–4	M	1560	39
	F	1500	37
5–6	M	1740	43
	F	1680	42
7–8	M	1980	49
	F	1900	47
9–11	M	2280	57
	F	2050	51
12–14	M	2640	66
	F	2150	53
15–17	M	2880	72
	F	2150	53

ADULTS

AGE RANGE YEARS	ACTIVITY	CALORIES	PROTEIN
MALE			
18–34	Sedentary	2510	63
	Moderately Active	2900	72
	Very active	3350	84
35–64	Sedentary	2400	60
	Mod. active	2750	69
	Very active	3350	84
65–74	Sedentary	2400	60
74+	Sedentary	2150	54
FEMALE			
18–54	Mod. active	2150	54
	Very active	2500	62
	Pregnancy	2400	60
	Lactation	2750	69
55–74	Sedentary	1900	47
74+	Sedentary	1680	42

nutrition (leading to obesity), for many recent research programmes show serious mineral deficiencies in our populations. Calcium, iron and zinc are the minerals that seem most often to be deficient. These are not isolated cases but are, unfortunately, commonplace. Even people who eat a carefully balanced diet have been found deficient in some minerals. And, in this country, research shows that one in four of our children is anaemic – they have iron deficiency.

Mineral deficiency is widespread. Yet, unlike vitamins, minerals are less easily damaged during cooking. They are also more abundant in our foods than vitamins – the notable exception being iron. However, they can be damaged by processing techniques and food refining.

So how much energy and protein?

After all this talk about what makes a healthier diet and how to achieve it, what do we actually *need*, in terms of calories (energy) and protein – the most important of all the nutrients that we get from our food if we are to be healthy?

The table opposite gives the recommended daily amount (RDA) following current medical and nutritional thinking.

	EVERYTHING YOU EVER WANTED TO	
MINERAL	**RDA**	**FUNCTION**
Iron	12mg* (F) 10mg* (M)	Vital for red blood cell formation.
Calcium	500mg*	Hardens bones. Necessary for tooth formation and normal activity of nerves and muscles. Controls blood cholesterol level, aids blood clotting.
Zinc	10mg*	Necessary for growth, sexual maturity, wound healing and sense of taste.
Magnesium	300mg*	Essential ingredient in bone. Needed for converting calories into energy, transmitting nerve impulses and muscle movement.
Potassium	3000mg	Needed to keep a normal fluid balance in cells, to maintain the acid/alkali balance of blood and for functioning of nervous system.

KEY: F = Female: M = Male   *UK Recommended Daily Amount

KNOW ABOUT MINERALS – AND MORE!

DEFICIENCY SYMPTOMS	BEST VEGETARIAN SOURCES	OTHER SOURCES
Tiredness, lethargy, malaise, anaemia, breathlessness.	Brewer's yeast, soya beans, soya flour, wheatbran, dried fruits, parsley, wholegrain cereals, wholemeal bread, haricot beans, green vegetables.	Liver, kidney, heart, game, mussels, cockles, winkles, sardines, herring, beef and lamb.
Rickets in children, osteoporosis, nervous problems, weak muscles.	Dairy products, green leafy vegetables, nuts, cereals, fruit, root vegetables, pulses.	Oily fish, canned fish.
Growth failure, loss of sense of taste, smell and appetite, hair loss, eczema, smelly feet.	Brewer's yeast, hard cheese, eggs, pulses, wholegrain cereals, rice, green leaf vegetables, potatoes, yogurt.	Liver, shellfish, fish and meat.
Weakness, tiredness, nervousness, palpitations, low blood sugar, muscle cramps, hyperactivity in children.	Brewer's yeast, dried peas, brown rice, nuts, soya beans, most vegetables, dried fruit, wholemeal products.	
Acute muscle weakness, paralysis, appetite loss, low blood pressure, drowsiness, vomiting.	Wholegrains, bran, wheatgerm, nuts, seeds, pulses, honey, dates, prunes, milk, brewer's yeast, dried fruits, beverages, cheese, vegetables, salads.	Fish.

EVERYTHING YOU EVER WANTED TO		
MINERAL	**RDA**	**FUNCTION**
Sodium	1200mg	Essential for muscle and nerve activity. Needed for water distribution through body.
Copper	2mg	Essential for manufacture of haemoglobin, growth in children.
Selenium	N/A	Maintains resistance to disease, healthy hair, skin, eyes and sight. Needed for healthy heart and liver. Protects against cancer.
Phosphorus	N/A	Needed for the building of bones and teeth. Involved in energy conversion.

KNOW ABOUT MINERALS – AND MORE!

DEFICIENCY SYMPTOMS	BEST VEGETARIAN SOURCES	OTHER SOURCES
Unlikely loss of appetite, weakness, mental apathy, dry mouth.	Yeast extract, cheese, tinned vegetables, most food except fruit.	Bacon, smoked fish, salami, cornflakes, processed meats, most foods.
Anaemia, irritability, water retention, brittle bones, loss of hair texture.	Brewer's yeast, olives, nuts, pulses, wholegrain cereals, dried fruit, green vegetables.	Liver, shellfish, meat, fish, poultry.
Muscular disease, heart disease, cancer.	Wholegrains, cereals, dairy products, fruit, vegetables.	Organ meats, fish and shellfish, muscle meats.
Appetite loss, weakness, bone pain, joint soreness, malaise, irritability, pins and needles, speech disorders.	Yeast extract, brewer's yeast, dried skimmed milk, wheatgerm, soya flour, hard cheese, nuts, wholegrain cereals, wholemeal bread, eggs, yogurt.	Canned fish, fresh fish, meat and poultry.

CHAPTER THREE

HELPING TO PREVENT DISEASE

'PREVENTION is better than cure' is a phrase I was brought up with. As a child I remember my mum packing me off to school with an apple, among other things, saying merrily 'an apple a day keeps the doctor away'. When the cooler autumn days began to merge into winter I was always given plenty of oranges to eat to 'ward off the colds'. My mum often tells how her mother used to prevent illness rearing its ugly head in the family by lining up all her many children in the kitchen to receive their daily doses of brimstone and treacle! Apparently this was regarded as a general health-giving potion. It certainly made an impression on Mum. All I can say is thank goodness for apples!

I have already stressed that a healthy diet will minimize the risks of contracting certain diseases, such as cancer and heart disease. To a large extent we can prevent these diseases of affluence. Two important questions remain. Can we do anything else to protect ourselves from these diseases? What do we do if we already have such a disease? The answer to both these questions is a positive one. Research is increasingly finding that certain nutrients do have a protective influence on our bodies. Not only can vitamins and minerals prevent disease, they can also effectively treat disease. A healthy diet is crucial, however, in this process. You really cannot eat a plateful of chips and hamburgers, pop in a vitamin/mineral pill and think you are protecting yourself from disease. You are not. A good healthy diet is the base on which to build.

But don't wait until it is too late – prevention is far, far better than a cure.

Remember that excessive doses of vitamins and minerals can be harmful and you should not take very high doses without medical supervision. Research has shown that certain vitamins and minerals are useful for preventing or treating certain diseases. However, I must stress that conventional treatment should not be abandoned but used in conjunction with these alternatives.

HEART DISEASE PREVENTION

The heart is merely a pump – albeit a very efficient one. It is a hollow muscle that beats around 100,000 times each day and night. There are many forms of heart disease. The big killer is coronary heart disease, caused by the arteries in the heart becoming blocked by cholesterol and fatty deposits. The medical term for this is atherosclerosis, literally hardening of the arteries. This means that the blood carrying nutrients and oxygen to the heart muscle is obstructed. If the blood cannot find another effective route to the muscle then part of the heart muscle dies. This is a heart attack, coronary or myocardial infarction – all these terms mean the same thing. If large areas of the heart are affected then the heart will stop completely.

The simple changes to your diet that I have suggested – reducing saturated fat, sugar and salt and increasing fibre – will minimize the risk of a heart attack. However, certain vitamins and minerals have been found to be particularly beneficial in both the prevention and treatment of heart disease. The protective vitamins are vitamin C and vitamin E, and the minerals are calcium, magnesium and potassium. Diets rich in these nutrients will offer some protection against heart disease.

CHOLESTEROL

A few years ago the medical profession was divided as to the importance of cholesterol in causing blocked arteries. Today there can be no doubt about it. Raised cholesterol levels are a major cause of heart disease. Cholesterol is a fatty substance that clings to the artery walls, thereby narrowing them. This not only restricts the blood flow but also makes the blood more prone to clotting. There are two main types of cholesterol, one of which is 'good' and one 'bad'. Low density lipoprotein, or LDL for short, is the trouble-maker. This is the one that blocks the arteries and causes the problems. The 'good' type, high density lipoprotein or HDL, actually reduces the bad type in the blood. So what we want is a high level of HDL and a low level of LDL as this will protect against heart disease.

Increasing the consumption of polyunsaturated fatty acids will tend to increase the level of HDL. Vitamin E has been shown to protect polyunsaturated fatty acids in the blood from being destroyed, so increasing the level of the 'good' HDL type of cholesterol. Raised blood cholesterol levels have been reduced by taking vitamin C or nicotinic acid (niacin) daily.

STROKES

A stroke is usually caused by atherosclerosis of brain arteries or high blood pressure. The brain is damaged and usually this results in paralysis down one side of the body. Once again a switch from saturated to polyunsaturated fatty acids is desirable. The vitamins C and E have also been shown to be useful both as a preventive measure and in treatment of the condition.

HIGH BLOOD PRESSURE

Blood pressure is the force generated by the blood within the system of arteries. When blood pressure is measured it is expressed by two figures. The first figure shows the 'systolic' pressure, the pressure of the blood leaving the heart. The second figure is the 'diastolic' pressure, the pressure in the artery itself. Blood pressure readings are expressed as the systolic over the diastolic. A normal reading would be about 120/80.

Many factors, such as narrowing of the arteries, weight gain and kidney problems, can cause the pressure of blood to rise. This is a problem because it can result in a heart attack or a stroke. In addition to a healthy diet a high ratio of potassium to sodium has been found very effective in reducing high blood pressure. A diet rich in potassium and low in sodium is, therefore, particularly useful in preventing or treating high blood pressure. Research studies have also shown that increasing the consumption of foods rich in the minerals calcium and magnesium can be beneficial.

CANCER PREVENTION

Cancer arises when cells divide in an abnormal and uncontrollable manner, which leads to the development of malignant cells. Cancer cells travel around the body in the bloodstream and this spreads the cancer to other parts of the body. Tumours that do not spread are called benign. Recent research indicates that cancer is made up of two stages. The first stage is 'initiation' and the second stage is 'promotion'. Carcinogenic (cancer forming) factors which are widespread in the environment, such as radiation and exhaust fumes, change the genetic blueprint of cells in the first stage. The second stage is then necessary if malignancy is to develop. Diet, especially high saturated fat intake, is considered to be the most important factor in this second stage of cancer.

In scientific trials vitamins A, C and E have been found to act as protectors against cancer. Vitamin A actually suppresses the formation of malignant cells while vitamins C and E block the formation of carcinogens from food. Calcium has been found to be of some use in the prevention of cancer of the colon. It acts like a sponge to absorb excess bile acids, caused by high fat intake, and thus protects the wall of the bowel. More recently, a trace mineral called selenium has been found to be of particular use in preventing *and* treating cancer. It appears that selenium acts in two ways. It boosts our own immune system, giving us extra protection from cancer, and also toughens the membranes of the cells making them less prone to attack.

Reducing the risk of these life-threatening diseases is possible by simply being aware of the 'good' and 'bad' foods in your diet and taking the appropriate action.

CHAPTER FOUR

THE PROOF OF THE PUDDING

ALL THE recipes contained in this book have one very important thing in common – they are good for your health. Each recipe is healthy in its own right: it provides nutrients, and is low in fat, salt and sugar and high in fibre. Each, therefore, falls in line with current thinking on healthy diets. By the way, when I use the word 'diet' I mean it in the broadest sense – the food we consume. As soon as you mention the word 'diet' most people assume that you are talking about slimming. I am not. However, you will find that with a healthy wholefood diet you will tend not to put on weight. In fact, if anything, you will lose any surplus weight you may have.

The recipes range from tempting starters to delicious desserts. There is something for everyone to try, from vegetarian foods to white meat and fish dishes. Variety is the name of the game. I see this book as providing another option. People don't have to be strictly cat-egorized as 'meat eaters' or 'vegetarians'. You can eat both vegetarian food and meat-based foods – they are not, as many people believe, mutually exclusive. The important factor is that you eat a diet which is healthier; and this means cutting down as much as possible on meat consumption. The recipes contained in this book provide you with the information and knowledge to do this effec-tively. And whether you choose vegetarian alternatives for all your meals or just two or three a week, you will be achieving a healthier diet for yourself and your family.

If you do consume meat always make sure that you

cook it with 'fat minimization' in mind. Trim the fat off any meat before you cook it. When cooking meat never let it stand in its own fat and juices – as you would in roasting and frying. Better ways to cook it would be grilling, baking on a trivet or steaming. These methods ensure that a lot of the fat content is 'cooked out' of the meat and can be thrown away. Never use this mixture of fat and juices for gravy as it is full of saturated fat and cholesterol. Remember that fish and white meats, such as chicken and turkey (but remove the skin before cooking as this is where most of the fat is contained), are far healthier than red meats.

THE RECIPES

You will be familiar with most of the ingredients used in the recipes. However, occasionally you may come across something which you have neither seen nor used before, such as tahini, which is sesame seed paste, silken tofu, which is a soyabean curd, concentrated soya milk and low-sodium baking powder. You may not find these on the supermarket shelves, although some large stores do stock them, but they are easily obtained from good healthfood shops.

Each of the recipes contains a row of symbols to tell you, at a glance, about freezing etc. And each recipe shows the calorie content per portion. The key to this row of symbols is:

F   Suitable for freezing   4   Number of servings
V   Suitable for vegetarians

SWAP SHOP RECIPES

You will find that each of the following chapters has examples of how you can convert traditional recipes to newer, healthier versions. Obviously this isn't necessary for things like salads – though keep away from the mayonnaise and salad cream – but I hope it will help you to understand the principles involved and enable you to convert favourite recipes.

MEASUREMENT EQUIVALENTS			
Grams (g)	Ounces (oz)	Millilitres (ml)	Fluid Ounces (fl. oz)
15	½		
25	1	25	1
40	1½	50	2
50	2	75	3
60	2½	125	4
75	3	150	5 (¼ pint)
100	4	175	6
125	4	200	7
150	5	225	8
175	6	250	10 (½ pint)
180	6½		
200	7	275	10 (½ pint)
225	8 (½lb)	300	11
250	9	350	12
275	10	375	13
300	11	400	15 (¾ pint)
350	12	425	16 (¾ pint)
375	13	450	17
400	14	475	18
425	15	500	20 (1 pint)
450	16 (1lb)	550	20 (1 pint)
475	17	850	30
500	18	1 litre	35
700	24 (1½lb)	1.1 litres	40 (2 pints)
1000 (1kg)	2 pounds	1.7 litres	60 (3 pints)

CENTIMETRES TO INCHES

Centimetres	Inches
6mm	¼in
1cm	½in
2.5cm	1in
5cm	2in
7.5cm	3in
10cm	4in
12.5cm	5in
15cm	6in
18cm	7in
20cm	8in
23cm	9in
25cm	10in
28cm	11in
30cm	12in

OVEN TEMPERATURES

Temperature	Centigrade (C)	Fahrenheit (F)	Gas Mark (GM)
	70	150	
	80	175	
	100	200	
Very Cool	110	225	¼
	120	250	½
	140	275	1
Cool	150	300	2
Warm	160	325	3
	180	350	4
Fairly Hot	190	375	5
	200	400	6
	220	425	7
Hot	230	450	8
Very Hot	240	475	9
	260	500	9

CONVERSION TABLES

If you're anything like me you will still be totally confused when trying to use metric weights and measures. I
still think in the old pounds and ounces. Throughout the

INGREDIENTS	
UK NAME	**AMERICAN NAME**
Aubergine	Egg plant
Courgette	Zucchini
Biscuits	Cookies
Onion	Bermuda Onion
Spring onion	Scallion
Marrow	Squash

NORTH AMERICAN MEASUREMENT EQUIVALENTS		
1 pint/575ml		2¼ cups
1oz /25g	margarine	2 tbsp
1oz /25g	flour	2 tbsp
1oz /25g	chopped seeds	2 tbsp
1oz /25g	grated cheese	4 tbsp
1lb /450g	breadcrumbs	8 cups
1lb /450g	rice (uncooked)	2 cups
1lb /450g	wholemeal flour	4 cups
1lb /450g	mashed potato	2 cups
1lb /450g	small beans	2 cups
1lb /450g	large beans	3 cups
1lb /450g	ground seeds	4 cups
1lb /450g	cottage cheese	2 cups
1lb /450g	soft cheese	2 cups

book, however, I have given both the metric and imperial measurements for weights and measurements. All you need to remember is to keep to either one or the other and you should be all right. The following table gives you the equivalents. And, as you will no doubt notice, for some of the imperial weights there are two possible metric equivalents. This metrication lark is so straightforward! You will find that in my recipes I sometimes use one of the equivalents and then sometimes the other. It all depends which is better for the particular recipe.

The tablespoons and teaspoons used in my recipes are the standard sizes 15ml and 5ml respectively, and are level, not heaped.

Ovens can vary enormously, and you will probably know any little quirks that yours has. It is important to remember that oven temperatures given in recipes are a guide. You know your oven better than anyone else, so if you know it is a particularly hot one it is best to set it slightly lower than the recipe suggests. And, of course, the reverse is equally true. If yours is a cool oven, up the temperature from that given in the recipe.

North American readers may be unfamiliar with some of our ingredients as we call them something different in the UK. These are all mentioned in the following recipes.

STOCK

The secret of many tasty, well-flavoured dishes lies in the stock that you use. Do avoid commercial stock cubes if you can; home-made stock, as in so many other things, is best and you can avoid using salt which bought stock cubes contain.

Onions, garlic, freshly ground black pepper and enough boiling water to cover them form the basis of all my stocks. Bring to the boil and then simmer until the vegetables are soft. If you want a thin stock strain off the vegetables and throw them away, and just use the liquid in which they have been cooked. For a thicker stock, perhaps for a casserole or thick soup, put the stock, vegetables and all, through a sieve or liquidizer. Although you can add other vegetables to the basic ingredients – leeks and carrots are good – avoid cabbage which can be unpleasantly strong and potatoes which are apt to break up.

CHAPTER FIVE

TEMPTING BEGINNINGS

To ME the starter is the most important part of any meal. Not because I particularly enjoy the starter more than the other courses but because it sets the tone for what is to follow. Remember the old saying 'first impressions are important'? It applies to food just as much as to anything else.

Any starter should tempt and tantalize the taste buds – hence the title of this chapter. It should make you long for the next course and not be looked upon as something to get through in order to progress to the rest of the meal. I always try to make interesting starters that intrigue people. But that does not mean that you have to spend ages preparing them. Most of the starters in this chapter are very easy and quick to make and freeze very well. What I tend to do is make double quantities of our favourites and freeze them – it makes life so much easier.

Soups remain the faithful standby for the vegetarian, but the scope is much wider than this. Remember that soups, especially when home-made, tend to be quite substantial and so only small portions are necessary. I love a nice hearty soup but then often find that I am too full to enjoy the main course! Many soups, if served with garlic bread or dumplings, are main courses in themselves and are wonderful served on a cold, wintry day. However, soups should not be limited to the cold winter months when the main ingredients are root crops. Summer soups are refreshing, served hot or chilled, and make use of seasonal vegetables such as spinach and lettuce.

In this chapter you will find some interesting soup recipes and also some tasty alternatives. For instance, vegetarian pâtés which rely on ingredients such as mushrooms and seeds rather than chicken livers. To many people a vegetarian pâté is unthinkable, but it isn't, as you'll see. These pâtés also make very good sandwich fillings and are useful served with salads as a main course or snack. Fish and white meat are also ideal for pâtés.

I cannot stress the importance of presentation often enough. Think of the plate, or dish, as a painting palette to be filled with either bursts of colour or gentle blends. And don't forget that textures and shapes make the dish even more interesting, both to look at and to eat.

COMMON PROBLEMS

The only problem associated with starters that I can think of is lack of imagination. A thick vegetable soup or chilled melon boat seem safe starters but are really terribly boring. Try making soups which are light, delicate and have a subtle blend of flavours. Think about serving chilled soups – they are wonderfully refreshing on a warm summer's day. For a change from eating wholemeal bread with the soup try hot poppyseed rolls (page 235). Melon is a good starter to any meal as it cleanses the palate and gets the taste buds ready for action. But chop it into chunks and combine it with other things, such as fruits, spices and cheeses, prawns and mackerel, instead of going for the traditional boat theme. It makes a welcome change.

SWAP SHOP RECIPES

Most people can make vegetable soups without any problem at all and not very much conversion is required. The obvious ingredient which needs changing for the vegetarian is chicken stock and you simply replace it with vegetable stock. However, more subtle changes are needed in some recipes which use cream and full-fat milk. But once again the changes are simple and do not detract from the taste.

Pâtés take a little bit more effort to convert but are well worth it. The meat element is easily replaced with ingredients such as mushrooms and pulses and the egg yolks are simply not needed. Tofu and low-fat soft cheeses are used instead of any cream listed in a recipe. The swap shop recipes in this chapter will give you a good idea of what I mean.

Cream of Barley Soup

(F V 4)
CALORIES: 188

Richard has always loved barley in soups and hot pots, which is a good thing as it is extremely good for the heart. Pot barley is unrefined pearl barley and therefore contains more nutrients and fibre.

PREPARATION TIME: 20 MINUTES
COOKING TIME: 100 MINUTES

INGREDIENTS: IMPERIAL/METRIC
2tbsp pot barley, washed
½pt/275ml vegetable stock
1 onion, peeled and chopped
½tsp celery seeds
1 bay leaf
1oz/25g polyunsaturated margarine (unhydrogenated)
2tbsp wholemeal flour
1pt soya milk (sugar free)
black pepper and low-sodium salt

METHOD
1　Simmer the barley in the stock for about 1 hour.
2　Add the onion, celery seeds and bay leaf and cook for a further 30 minutes.
3　Melt the margarine in a saucepan and add the flour. Cook for 1 minute, stirring.
4　Remove from the heat and gradually stir in the milk.
5　Add to the barley mixture.
6　Remove the bay leaf.
7　Reheat, stirring, and season. Serve with garlic bread.

Turkey Soup

(F 4)
CALORIES: 231

A creamy turkey soup without the cream and calories!
Tofu makes the soup taste really rich and packs in lots
and lots of important nutrients. This is a good way of
using up left-over turkey – especially at Christmastime.

PREPARATION TIME: 5 MINUTES
COOKING TIME: 10 MINUTES

INGREDIENTS: IMPERIAL/METRIC
8oz/225g turkey meat, cooked and skin removed
1tbsp olive oil
1 onion, peeled and grated
1pt/550ml chicken stock
¼pt/150ml silken tofu, liquidized
1tbsp fresh parsley, chopped
black pepper, freshly ground

METHOD ·
1   Cut the turkey meat into bite-size pieces.
2   Heat the oil and fry the onion for 2 minutes. Add the
    stock and bring to the boil. Simmer for 5 minutes.
3   Add the turkey and simmer for 3 minutes. Stir in the
    tofu and heat through – about 1 minute only. Season
    with black pepper, sprinkle with parsley and serve.

Vichyssoise

(F V 4)

PREPARATION TIME: 15 MINUTES
COOKING TIME: 35 MINUTES

INGREDIENTS: IMPERIAL/METRIC

Traditional Recipe
CALORIES: 451

2oz/50g butter
3 leeks, washed and chopped
1 onion, peeled and chopped
1lb/450g potatoes, peeled and chopped
1½pts/850ml chicken stock
½pt/275ml single cream
salt
pepper

Swap Shop Recipe
CALORIES: 303

2tbsp olive oil
3 leeks, washed and chopped
1 onion, peeled and chopped
1lb/450g potatoes, washed and chopped
1½pts/850ml vegetable stock
low-sodium salt
black pepper
½pt/275ml silken tofu, liquidized

METHOD
1　Heat the oil in a large saucepan and gently fry the
leeks and onion for about 3 minutes.

2 Add the potatoes, stock, salt and pepper. Cover and simmer for about 30 minutes until the potatoes are soft.
3 Remove from the heat and stir in the liquidized tofu.
4 Blend the soup until smooth.
5 Serve either hot or cold.

Leek and Butter Bean Soup

(F V 4)
CALORIES: 94

Leeks and butter beans go particularly well together and the rosemary adds a lovely aromatic quality.

PREPARATION TIME: 30 MINUTES
COOKING TIME: 75 MINUTES

INGREDIENTS: IMPERIAL/METRIC
1oz/25g polyunsaturated margarine (unhydrogenated)
1 onion, peeled and chopped
2 leeks, washed carefully and sliced
4oz/125g butter beans, soaked and drained
1tbsp dried rosemary
1½pts/850ml vegetable stock (unsalted)
4tbsp concentrated soya milk (sugar free)
black pepper and low-sodium salt
watercress to garnish

METHOD
1 Melt the margarine in a large saucepan and fry the onion and leeks for about 10 minutes.
2 Add the beans, rosemary and stock.

3   Bring to the boil and simmer for 1 hour, until the
     beans are cooked.
4   Add the concentrated soya milk and liquidize until
     smooth.
5   Add the seasoning.
6   Reheat and serve garnished with watercress.

Lettuce Soup

(F V 4)
CALORIES: 152

A very economical soup to make in summer when let-
tuces are plentiful. A delicate green in colour, the soup
looks very attractive with the spring onions sprinkled on
the top. Can be eaten hot or chilled.

PREPARATION TIME: 20 MINUTES
COOKING TIME: 55 MINUTES

INGREDIENTS: IMPERIAL/METRIC
2oz/50g polyunsaturated margarine (unhydrogenated)
12oz/350g lettuce leaves, washed and chopped
4 spring onions, washed and chopped
1tbsp wholemeal flour
1pt/550ml vegetable stock
¼pt/150ml soya milk
black pepper and low-sodium salt

METHOD
1   Melt the margarine in a large saucepan and fry the
     lettuce and all but a teaspoon of the chopped spring
     onions for 5 minutes.

2 Stir in the flour and add the stock.
3 Bring to the boil and simmer for 45 minutes, covered.
4 Liquidize the soup until smooth.
5 Add the soya milk and seasoning.
6 Reheat, but do not boil.
7 Serve hot with the remaining chopped spring onions scattered on top.

Parsnip and Lemon Soup

(F V 8)
CALORIES: 124

I invented this recipe when planning a dinner party with lemons as the theme of the meal. It proved to be very successful. It is pale lemon in colour, looks very sophisticated and the flavours are delicate.

PREPARATION TIME: 30 MINUTES
COOKING TIME: 45 MINUTES

INGREDIENTS. IMPERIAL/METRIC
2oz/50g polyunsaturated margarine (unhydrogenated)
1 onion, peeled and sliced
1lb/450g parsnips, peeled and cubed
8oz/225g potatoes, washed and cubed
2 garlic cloves, peeled and crushed
2pts/1.1l vegetable stock
2tsp saffron or turmeric
black pepper
1 lemon, zest and juice
¼pt/150ml silken tofu, liquidized
chopped parsley to garnish

METHOD

1 Melt the margarine in a large saucepan and cook the onion gently until soft, about 5 minutes.
2 Add the parsnips, potatoes and garlic. Cover and cook slowly for 20 minutes – until the vegetables are just soft.
3 Add stock, saffron (or turmeric) and pepper.
4 Bring to the boil and simmer for 10 minutes.
5 Add the lemon zest and juice.
6 Liquidize the soup until smooth.
7 Return to the pan and stir in the tofu.
8 Reheat without boiling.
9 Serve garnished with chopped parsley.

TIP BOX

Try using different herbs and spices in the recipes –
it really changes the flavour of the dish.

Garlic and Tofu Dip

(v 4)
CALORIES: 27

Garlic and tofu blend beautifully together and this makes a nice party dip. Add some wholemeal breadcrumbs if you prefer a firmer dip.

PREPARATION TIME: 5 MINUTES

INGREDIENTS: IMPERIAL/METRIC
2 garlic cloves, peeled and crushed
2oz/50g onion, peeled and finely chopped
¼pt/150ml silken tofu, liquidized
black pepper

METHOD
1   Combine all the ingredients well.
2   Serve chilled with raw vegetables.

Herb Dip

(F V 8)
CALORIES: 68

This dip looks very attractive with the chopped green herbs contrasting with the pale yellow of the cheeses.

PREPARATION TIME: 15 MINUTES

INGREDIENTS: IMPERIAL/METRIC
1tbsp fresh mint, chopped
1tbsp fresh parsley, chopped
4oz/125g low-fat vegetarian cheese, grated
4oz/125g low-fat vegetarian cottage cheese
4oz/125g low-fat vegetarian soft cheese
2 garlic cloves, peeled and crushed

METHOD
1   Combine all the ingredients well.
2   Serve chilled piled on top of curly endive leaves.

Hummus

(F V 4)
CALORIES: 252

This is a light hummus because I don't add any extra oil,
so you simply taste the chick peas and garlic.

PREPARATION TIME: 15 MINUTES

INGREDIENTS: IMPERIAL/METRIC
8oz/225g chick peas, washed and soaked overnight
1tbsp lemon juice
1tbsp tahini
2 garlic cloves, peeled and crushed
black pepper and low-sodium salt
a little water to aid the liquidizing process

METHOD
1 Cook the chick peas in water for about 1 hour until
   tender.
2 Drain the chick peas, reserving 2 tablespoons of the
   liquid.
3 Place the liquid, lemon juice, tahini, garlic and chick
   peas in a blender and blend until smooth.
4 Season to taste.
5 Serve chilled piled on top of red cabbage or lettuce
   leaves.

Fresh Salmon Pâté

(F 6)

This is a lovely delicate pâté with a fine texture and is enhanced by serving with watercress and orange. Any kind of fish can be used instead of the salmon – although for a special occasion it is worth the expense.

PREPARATION TIME: 35 MINUTES
COOKING TIME: 40 MINUTES

INGREDIENTS: IMPERIAL/METRIC

Traditional Recipe
CALORIES: 642

12oz/350g fresh salmon
1 onion, peeled and sliced
1 carrot, peeled and sliced
2 bay leaves
¼pt/150ml white wine
8oz/225g unsalted butter, creamed

SAUCE
3oz/75g butter
3oz/75g white flour
1pt/575ml milk
2tsp lemon juice
salt and pepper

GARNISH
3 hard-boiled eggs, sliced

Swap Shop Recipe
CALORIES: 569

12oz/350g fresh salmon
1 onion, peeled and sliced
1 carrot, scraped and sliced
2 bay leaves
¼pt/150ml white wine
4oz/125g polyunsaturated margarine (unhydrogenated)

SAUCE
3oz/75g polyunsaturated margarine (unhydrogenated)
3oz/75g wholemeal flour
1pt/575ml skimmed milk
2tsp lemon juice
black pepper

GARNISH
½ cucumber, thinly sliced

METHOD

1   Place the salmon in a large saucepan with the onion, carrot, bay leaves and wine. Add just enough water to cover. Bring to the boil and simmer for 20 minutes. Remove from the heat.

2   Make the sauce by melting the margarine in a saucepan. Add the flour and cook for 1 minute, stirring all the time. Remove from the heat and gradually stir in the milk. Bring gently to the boil and simmer for about 3 minutes before adding the lemon juice and pepper. Leave to cool.

3   Skin and carefully flake the fish, removing all the bones, and place it in a food processor for 1 minute.

4   When all the ingredients are cool, mix together the salmon, sauce and margarine. Place the pâté in a dish and cover with foil until you are ready to garnish it.

5   Arrange the cucumber slices in ever-decreasing circles on the top of the pâté. Chill and serve when required.

Smoked Trout Pâté

(F 4)
CALORIES: 183

Smoked fish tastes marvellous and gives that special something to a pâté. To ring the changes why not give smoked mackerel a try – it's equally as nice as smoked trout!

PREPARATION TIME: 15 MINUTES
CHILLING TIME: 3 HOURS

INGREDIENTS: IMPERIAL/METRIC
6oz/175g smoked trout, skinned and boned
2oz/50g polyunsaturated margarine (unhydrogenated)
2tbsp fromage frais
1 lemon, zest and juice
½tsp anchovy essence
black pepper

METHOD
1   Flake the smoked trout.
2   Beat the margarine with the fromage frais, lemon zest and juice, anchovy essence and black pepper.
3   Stir in the smoked trout.
4   Chill the pâté for 3 hours.

Soft Lentil Pâté

(F V 4)
CALORIES: 197

A soft pâté which is popular with our guests. Hot poppy-seed rolls (page 235) or wholemeal toast complement it nicely.

PREPARATION TIME: 20 MINUTES
COOKING TIME: 30 MINUTES

INGREDIENTS: IMPERIAL/METRIC
6oz/175g continental (small brown) lentils
1oz/25g polyunsaturated margarine (unhydrogenated)
1 onion, peeled and chopped
6oz/175g mushrooms, wiped and sliced
1tsp dried chives
1tsp dried marjoram
1tsp lemon juice
black pepper and low-sodium salt

METHOD
1 Cook the lentils in boiling water until soft, about 20 minutes. Drain well.
2 Meanwhile, melt the margarine and fry the onion until soft, about 5 minutes.
3 Add the mushrooms and fry for 2 minutes, stirring.
4 Add the remaining ingredients and mix well.
5 Pile into ramekin dishes and serve well chilled, garnished with, for example, watercress leaves.

Mushrooms and Seed Pâté

(F V 8)
CALORIES: 177

A tasty and versatile pâté: you can change the subtle flavours by using different herbs – rosemary is particularly nice. And use whatever seeds you happen to have (sunflower seeds are always a good standby).

PREPARATION TIME: 30 MINUTES
COOKING TIME: 60 MINUTES
TEMPERATURE: 180°C/350°F/GAS 4

INGREDIENTS: IMPERIAL/METRIC
2oz/50g polyunsaturated margarine (unhydrogenated)
1 large onion, peeled and chopped
1lb/450g mushrooms, wiped and sliced
8oz/225g wholemeal breadcrumbs
4oz/125g seeds, ground
1 egg white
1tbsp tahini
1tsp yeast extract
1tbsp dried mixed herbs
black pepper and low-sodium salt

METHOD
1 Grease and line a 1lb/450g loaf tin.
2 Melt the margarine and fry the onion for 5 minutes until soft.
3 Add the mushrooms and cook until the liquid evaporates.
4 Liquidize the mixture.
5 Add all the remaining ingredients and mix well.
6 Pour the mixture into the prepared tin.

7   Cover with greased foil and cook for about 1 hour.
8   Allow to cool for at least 10 minutes before turning out.

Vegetable Pâté

(F V 8)
CALORIES: 122

This pâté is pale green in colour and has a lovely creamy texture.

PREPARATION TIME: 45 MINUTES
COOKING TIME: 30 MINUTES
TEMPERATURE: 180°C/350°C/GAS 4

INGREDIENTS: IMPERIAL/METRIC
2lb/1kg courgettes, washed and grated
1tbsp sea salt
2oz/50g polyunsaturated margarine (unhydrogenated)
1 onion, peeled and chopped
3 garlic cloves, peeled and crushed
2tsp mustard
2tbsp fresh herbs, chopped
black pepper and low-sodium salt
½pt/250ml silken tofu, liquidized
4 egg whites, whisked until stiff
4oz/125g broccoli, washed and lightly steamed
pinch cayenne pepper

METHOD

1 Grease and line a 2lb/900g loaf tin.
2 Place the grated courgettes in a colander and sprinkle with the salt. Leave to drain for 30 minutes. Rinse under cold running water and then leave to drain again.
3 Melt the margarine and fry the onion and garlic for 5 minutes. Add the courgettes and cook for 10 minutes. Stir well.
4 Remove from the heat and cool slightly.
5 Add the courgette mixture, mustard, herbs and the seasoning to the tofu.
6 Carefully fold in the egg whites.
7 Pour half the courgette mixture into the prepared tin.
8 Place the broccoli in a layer over the courgettes.
9 Pour over the remaining courgette mixture.
10 Cover the tin with foil and stand in a roasting tin which has 2in/5cm of cold water in it.
11 Cook for 1 hour 15 minutes.
12 Chill in tin. Turn out and serve garnished with tomato slices and watercress leaves.

TIP BOX

You can make the pâté look and taste different by layering it. Alternate the pâté with layers of tomatoes, mushrooms or low-fat cheeses.

Smoked Mackerel Ramekins

(F 4)
CALORIES: 188

This makes a nice starter served with wholemeal toast and spring onions.

PREPARATION TIME: 15 MINUTES
COOKING TIME: 5 MINUTES

INGREDIENTS: IMPERIAL/METRIC
2 smoked mackerel fillets, skinned and boned
½oz/15g polyunsaturated margarine (unhydrogenated)
½oz/15g plain wholemeal flour
½pt/275ml skimmed milk
1½oz/40g Edam cheese, grated
black pepper
good pinch freshly grated nutmeg

METHOD
1   Flake the mackerel into small pieces.
2   Melt the margarine, stir in the flour and cook gently for 1 minute. Remove from the heat and gradually stir in the milk. Bring slowly to the boil and continue to cook until the sauce thickens, stirring continuously. Remove from the heat.
3   Stir in the cheese and seasonings. Add the fish and divide the mixture between four ramekin dishes. Serve immediately.

Tuna Mousse

(6)

CALORIES: 181

This tuna mousse looks and tastes impressive and yet it is very easy to prepare. If you can't get Gelozone use gelatine or agar-agar instead.

PREPARATION TIME: 30 MINUTES
COOKING TIME: 5 MINUTES
CHILLING TIME: 2 HOURS

INGREDIENTS: IMPERIAL/METRIC
½pt/275ml fish stock
1oz/25g onion, peeled and chopped
2 garlic cloves, crushed
1 tsp fresh rosemary, chopped
7oz/200g tin tuna in brine, drained and flaked
3tsp Gelozone (see note above)
4tbsp fromage frais

METHOD

1 Warm the fish stock and add the onion, garlic, rosemary and tuna. Stir well.

2 Sprinkle on the Gelozone and stir vigorously with a fork but do not allow to boil. Once the mixture begins to steam remove from the heat and leave to cool slightly.

3 Place the mixture in a blender and blend until fairly smooth.

4 Gently fold the fromage frais into the tuna mixture.

5 Pour the mixture into a 1pt/600ml pudding basin or mould, cover with foil and leave in a refrigerator until it sets – about 2 hours. Turn out and serve.

Hot Chicken Mousse

(F 6)

This beautiful hot chicken mousse tastes wonderfully rich and served with some wholemeal toast makes a substantial start to the meal.

PREPARATION TIME: 25 MINUTES
COOKING TIME: 50 MINUTES
TEMPERATURE: 220°C/425°F/GAS 7

INGREDIENTS: IMPERIAL/METRIC

Traditional Recipe
CALORIES: 285

1oz/25g butter
1oz/25g plain flour
3oz/75g luncheon meat
3oz/75g breadcrumbs
2 eggs, separated
2tbsp parsley, chopped
2tbsp Parmesan cheese, grated
salt and pepper

SAUCE
3tbsp double cream
3tbsp mayonnaise
¼tsp lemon juice
1tbsp chopped chives

Swap Shop Recipe

CALORIES: 158

1oz/25g polyunsaturated margarine (unhydrogenated)
1oz/25g wholemeal flour, plain
½pt/275ml skimmed milk
black pepper
3oz/75g cooked chicken, chopped
3oz/75g wholemeal breadcrumbs
1 egg yolk
2tbsp chopped parsley
2tbsp Gouda cheese, grated
2 egg whites

SAUCE
3tbsp low-fat natural yogurt
3tbsp low-fat mayonnaise
¼tsp lemon juice
1tbsp chopped chives

METHOD

1 Lightly grease and line a 1lb/450g loaf tin with greaseproof paper. Melt the margarine in a saucepan and stir in the flour. Cook for 1 minute. Remove from the heat and gradually add the milk. Stirring continuously, bring to the boil and add the seasoning and chicken. Simmer for 5 minutes.

2 Beat the breadcrumbs, egg yolk, parsley and cheese into the chicken mixture. Whisk the egg whites until stiff and carefully fold in.

3 Spoon the mixture into the prepared loaf tin and level the surface. Cover with a piece of lightly greased foil.

4 Stand in a roasting tin and add enough hot water to come halfway up the sides of the loaf tin. Bake for about 45 minutes until the mousse is set.

5   Meanwhile, make the sauce by mixing together the
     yogurt, low-fat mayonnaise, lemon juice and chives.
     Cover and chill until you are ready to serve.
6   Allow the mousse to settle for 10 minutes then turn
     out of the tin on to a warm serving dish and slice to
     serve.

Chicken Parcels

(F 4)
CALORIES: 151

The combination of chicken, cheese and juniper berries
works very well and once encased in lightly steamed
lettuce leaves looks delightful – not to mention quite
impressive!

PREPARATION TIME: 20 MINUTES
COOKING TIME: 30 minutes
TEMPERATURE: 220°C/425°F/GAS 7

INGREDIENTS: IMPERIAL/METRIC
4 lettuce leaves, large
2 chicken breasts, skinned and boned
6 juniper berries, crushed
4oz/125g Edam or Gouda cheese, grated
½tsp nutmeg, freshly grated
black pepper

METHOD
1   Steam the lettuce leaves for a few seconds and place
     them under cold running water for 1 minute to fix
     their colour.

2   Lay each leaf flat on a work surface and cut out the tough central stalk.

3   Cut each chicken breast in half. Place a piece of chicken in the centre of each lettuce leaf and sprinkle with the juniper berries, grated cheese, nutmeg and black pepper.

4   Wrap the lettuce leaves around the chicken to make neat parcels.

5   Lay them in a lightly oiled ovenproof dish and cover with foil. Cook for about 30 minutes until the chicken is tender.

Potted Chicken

(F 4)
CALORIES: 135

Little pots of minced chicken bound together with fromage frais – what a winning combination. The addition of the lemon zest gives a welcome zing to the dish.

PREPARATION TIME: 5 MINUTES

INGREDIENTS: IMPERIAL/METRIC
12oz/350g chicken meat, cooked and skinned
1 lemon, zest of
1 tsp fresh tarragon, finely chopped
black pepper
2oz/50g fromage frais

METHOD
1   Mince the chicken meat finely.

2   Add the lemon zest and tarragon. Season to taste with the black pepper.

3   Stir in the fromage frais and mix together well.
4   Divide the mixture into four ramekin dishes and press firmly. Leave to firm up in the refrigerator until you are ready to serve them.

Tomato Moulds

(v 4)
CALORIES: 43

These bright little moulds look mouthwatering with the different vegetables and seeds suspended in the bright red of the tomato 'jelly'. I use Gelozone as the setting agent instead of the traditional gelatine which contains animal extracts.

PREPARATION TIME: 20 MINUTES
COOKING TIME: 5 MINUTES
SETTING TIME: 30 MINUTES

INGREDIENTS: IMPERIAL/METRIC
¼pt/150ml tomato juice
1tsp Gelozone
1 stick celery, washed and chopped
1oz/25g onion, grated
2oz/50g sunflower seeds
1oz/25g watercress, washed and chopped
1tbsp fresh mint, washed and chopped
black pepper

METHOD
1   Pour the tomato juice into a saucepan and heat gently.

2   Sprinkle on the Gelozone and whisk in until well blended.

3   Stir and continue to heat until the juice begins to steam – do not allow to boil.

4   Remove from the heat and add all the remaining ingredients, stirring well.

5   Spoon the mixture into individual moulds (I use small, round, plastic moulds) and leave to set in the fridge for about 30 minutes.

6   Turn out on to a serving plate with a garnish of your choice.

Melon, Cheese and Ginger Refresher

(v 8)
CALORIES: 58

Wonderfully simple to make and delicious to eat. The sweet, juicy melon combines beautifully with the textures of the ginger and the apple.

PREPARATION TIME: 10 MINUTES

INGREDIENTS: IMPERIAL/METRIC
½ melon, chopped
8oz/225g low-fat cottage cheese
1oz/25g preserved ginger, chopped finely
1 red apple, washed well and chopped
black pepper
8 chicory leaves
8 sprigs fresh mint
paprika pepper

METHOD

1 Combine the first five ingredients.
2 Pile into tall elegant glasses and garnish with the chicory leaves and mint sprigs.
3 Sprinkle a little paprika pepper on top of each one.

TIP BOX

If you prefer your pâté to have a smoother consistency, just liquidize for a little longer.

CHAPTER SIX

SOMETHING FISHY ...

FISH IS the perfect food in many ways. For one thing it's very fast to cook – the original fast food! And it is easily cooked by anyone, no experience necessary – as the advertisements go. Once you add the exceptionally high nutritional value of fish you really are on to a winner.

The variety of fish now available to the consumer is wide, which also means that the price tags can accommodate any budget, small or large. That's got to be good news. I can remember a time, not too long ago, when it was a real effort to buy fresh fish in the little town near to where I lived. It was almost impossible to track it down and when I did, I was left with the haddock or cod decision. How things have changed. Fresh fish is back in favour and can be bought from supermarkets, grocery shops, as well as from fishmongers, and sometimes even from local village post offices! And what about the choice available to us now? I will go into town armed with a list of fish that I want to buy and then what happens? I see a whole array of fish laid out before me and my carefully prepared list goes out of the window – along with the recipes they were intended for. I just can't resist unfamiliar fish and I'm sure that George, my fishmonger, does it on purpose!

FISH FACT FILE

Generally speaking there are five groups of fish:

- round white fish – haddock and mullet;
- flat white fish – plaice and sole;
- fatty (oily) fish – mackerel and herring;
- shellfish – prawns and crab;
- cartilaginous (boneless) – monkfish and huss.

Buying Guide
When buying fresh fish you should be looking for:

- bright, clear eyes that are not sunken;
- firm flesh;
- bright skin that isn't slimy;
- blood-red gills;
- firmly attached scales.

Shellfish need to:

- have their shells intact;
- have a heavy feel for their size;
- be chilled.

Smoked fish should be:

- bright and glossy;
- firm to the touch and never soggy;
- naturally smoked.

Cooking Guide
Although fish is probably the easiest of foods to cook, it still helps to have a few golden rules in mind.

- Cook as soon as possible after purchase.
- Never overcook.

- Always preheat the oven or grill.
- Don't keep warm, but serve immediately.

Fish is versatile: it can be poached, baked, roasted, steamed, grilled, barbecued, braised, microwaved and, dare I say it, even fried! Frying is still a popular way to cook fish in Britain but it doesn't have to be a health hazard. Stir-frying, using a little of the right type of oil, is quite a healthy way to cook fish. A useful addition to any kitchen are the newly available fat-free fryers which reduce to a minimum the amount of fat needed.

For me a flavoursome fish, such as monkfish, served with a rich creamy sauce, takes some beating, although I also love the taste and texture of a salmon steak, microwaved or grilled with just a sprinkling of black pepper. And barbecued fish kebabs are simply mouthwatering. With fish you really can't go wrong. There are plenty of recipes in this chapter, ranging from fish curries to fish pies, to tempt the taste buds.

Nutritional guide

The nutritional value of fish is beyond question. They are an excellent source of good quality protein and minerals. All fish contain phosphorus and sea fish are a valuable source of iodine. And, with fish such as sardines and herrings where the bones are often eaten, the calcium content is high. White fish are invaluable to slimmers as the fat content is minimal: a perfect low-calorie, high-protein food. All fish contain B vitamins but, nutritionally speaking, fatty fish are superior to white, containing more energy, and also fat-soluble vitamins A, D and E, and iron. Fatty fish are 5–30 per cent fat and this type of fat is good for you. Polyunsaturated fatty acids are known to inhibit the tendency of blood to clot and thus reduce the risk of heart disease and strokes. Including fatty fish in the diet is, for this reason alone, beneficial. The fatty-fish group includes eel, herring, bloater, kipper, mackerel, pilchard, salmon, sardines, sprats, trout, tuna and whitebait.

COMMON PROBLEMS

Fish sometimes has a bad image. To many people a fish meal conjures up memories of school dinners in all their glory. Barely warm, colourless and flavourless fried fish served with equally colourless and flavourless mashed potato. The school-dinner syndrome was important in framing my opinion of fish and it took me a long time to want to eat it again. Looking back on those school dinners, I now see it was quite a skill to cook all the flavour and texture out of the fish – I just don't know how they managed it. Pure genius!

But now I love eating fish in all its forms and when I think of a fish meal my mind whisks back to a tiny Greek taverna on the then unspoilt island of Skiathos. The only choice on the menu was 'big fish' or 'little fish'. Richard and I both decided on the big fish. And sure enough the fish were big and we had two of them – each! They were simply cooked, grilled with fresh herbs, and served with a large Greek salad. That was the best fish dish that I have ever tasted – the hot sunshine on our backs, the cool white wine and breathtaking views had no part to play in it (she says with a smile on her face!)

Fish and chips with salt, vinegar and scraps wrapped in last week's newspaper is another traditional image. It is hard to break away from this and see fish as a healthy, interesting, versatile food just as worthy of a dinner party as the most expensive of steaks. There does seem to be a general problem with overcooking fish. We tend to believe that fish cannot be cooked in less than ten minutes, and the result is often dried-out fish with the texture of rubber. Unlike meat, fish does not have any connective tissue and therefore is not tough. The cooking process is merely to cook the fish and not to tenderize it. Fish should be succulent, juicy and tasty.

Many people (and I am one of them) dislike fish because of the bones. An easy way around the problem is to avoid particularly bony fish, such as kippers and herring. Or instead of buying fish whole, buy steaks where you get only the central bone which is easily discarded. I eat a lot of cartilaginous fish, such as monkfish, as they contain no bones at all, taste delicious and have a good firm texture. So that's what to do when you don't want to spend ages sorting out the flesh from the bones and piling the 'uneatables' on a separate plate!

SWAP SHOP RECIPES

The main problem area here will be fish dishes that require a sauce, as many recipes do. The main ingredients that need swapping are butter and cream. So instead simply use a polyunsaturated margarine that is also unhydrogenated, and fromage frais, tofu or yogurt. Not only will this greatly reduce the calorie content of the dish, but it will also make it far healthier. When a bechamel sauce is called for, try using a wholemeal or malted granary flour instead of the white normally used. The taste is enhanced by the nutty flavour of the flour. Full-fat cheeses in sauces can be replaced by low-fat alternatives such as Edam and Gouda, and by half-fat varieties.

Many people still like to fry fish and you can make this a healthier meal by minimizing the fat. Instead of deep-frying you could shallow-fry, stir-fry or use a fat-free frying pan. Be aware of the type of fat you are using. Don't use saturated fat or polyunsaturated fat to fry – try olive oil or any other mono-unsaturated oil. Make sure that the fat is really hot before adding the fish because it seals the flesh quickly and less fat is absorbed. Have some pieces of kitchen paper ready to blot the excess fat off the fish once you have finished cooking. By using these methods you can still eat your fried fish and retain a relatively healthy diet. Or cook the fish totally fat-free by a method such as steaming or poaching in stock. It really is easy to cook healthily with fish as the main ingredient.

Fish Wellington

(F 8)

CALORIES: 227

Perfect for a dinner party. Layers of light filo pastry encasing haddock fillets stuffed with pâté and mushrooms. What a beautiful meal!

PREPARATION TIME: 40 MINUTES
COOKING TIME: 30 MINUTES
TEMPERATURE: 220°C/425°F/GAS 7

INGREDIENTS: IMPERIAL/METRIC
1tbsp olive oil
2oz/50g onion, chopped finely
4oz/125g button mushrooms, wiped and chopped
1 recipe smoked mackerel pâté (see page 71; substitute
mackerel for trout)
4tbsp fromage frais
8 filo pastry sheets
little olive oil for brushing
2 large haddock fillets, skinned and boned
black pepper

METHOD

1 Heat the oil and gently fry the onion and mushrooms until soft.

2 Add the onion and mushroom mixture to the smoked mackerel pâté and mix well. Add the fromage frais.

3 Lightly oil each sheet of filo pastry and place them, one on top of the other, on a lightly oiled baking sheet.

4 Place one of the haddock fillets in the centre of the pastry and sprinkle with black pepper.

5   Spread the mackerel mixture on top and cover with
    the other haddock fillet.
6   Gather up the pastry and form a rope effect down the
    centre of the pie – this will seal the fish inside.
7   Lightly brush with oil and bake for about 30
    minutes.

Fish Pie

(F 6)
CALORIES: 402

A fish pie with a difference!

PREPARATION TIME: 30 MINUTES
COOKING TIME: 40 MINUTES
TEMPERATURE: 190°C/375°F/GAS 5

INGREDIENTS: IMPERIAL/METRIC
4oz/125g smoked salmon *or* smoked mackerel
4oz/125g herring, skinned, boned and lightly steamed
4oz/125g tuna, canned in brine and drained
4oz/125g prawns, cooked and peeled
8oz/250g button mushrooms, wiped
2oz/50g polyunsaturated margarine (unhydrogenated)
¼pt/150ml fish stock
¼pt/150ml fromage frais
1 lemon, zest of
black pepper
freshly grated nutmeg
2 egg whites, whisked
8 filo pastry sheets
olive oil for brushing

METHOD

1 Thinly slice the smoked salmon or mackerel. Finely mince the herring, tuna and prawns and mix with the mushrooms and margarine.

2 Add the stock, fromage frais and lemon zest.

3 Stir in the black pepper and nutmeg and fold in the egg whites.

4 Line an 8in/20cm flan ring with half the filo pastry sheets – lightly brush each sheet with oil as you use it. As you line the flan case make sure that the pastry overlaps the sides evenly.

5 Spread the mixture into the flan case and press down firmly.

6 Place the remaining filo pastry sheets on top of the flan case – again lightly oil each one as you use it. Gather up the excess pastry overlapping the flan case, twist it around like a rope and seat it on the edge of the pie.

7 Cook until golden brown and crispy, about 40 minutes.

Trout in Cream

(F 4)

The yogurt gives the trout a lovely tangy flavour which is accentuated by the lemon juice.

PREPARATION TIME: 10 MINUTES
COOKING TIME: 20 MINUTES
TEMPERATURE: 180°C/350°F/GAS 4

INGREDIENTS: IMPERIAL/METRIC

Traditional Recipe
CALORIES: 296

4 trout, cleaned
1 lemon, juice of
1tbsp fresh chives, chopped
1tbsp fresh parsley, chopped
1tbsp water
¼pt/150ml fresh cream
2tbsp breadcrumbs
2oz/50g butter

Swap Shop Recipe
CALORIES: 187

4 trout, cleaned
1 lemon, juice of
1tbsp fresh chives, chopped
1tbsp fresh parsley, chopped
1tbsp water
¼pt/150ml natural low-fat yogurt
2tbsp wholemeal breadcrumbs
1oz/25g polyunsaturated margarine (unhydrogenated)

METHOD

1 Lay the fish in a lightly greased ovenproof dish – preferably a shallow one.

2 Sprinkle over the lemon juice, herbs and water. Cover with foil and cook for 20 minutes until the fish is tender.

3 Heat the yogurt gently and pour over the fish. Sprinkle with the breadcrumbs and dot with the margarine.

4 Place under a hot grill for a few minutes to brown.

Fish Kebabs

(4–6)
CALORIES: 350

Any shellfish or fish can be used for these kebabs as long as it is firm. The marinade adds a whole new dimension to the recipe.

PREPARATION TIME: 35 MINUTES
+MARINATING TIME OF 2 HOURS
COOKING TIME: 20 MINUTES

INGREDIENTS: IMPERIAL/METRIC
1lb/450g firm white fish, skinned and boned
1 green pepper, washed, seeded and cut into squares
8oz/225g prawns, cooked and peeled
8oz/225g button mushrooms
8oz/225g tomatoes, sliced very thickly
bay leaves

MARINADE
1tbsp olive oil
1 bunch spring onions, finely chopped
3 garlic cloves, crushed
4fl oz/100ml fish stock
1 lemon, juice and zest
1tbsp parsley, chopped
1tsp tarragon, chopped
6 juniper berries, crushed

METHOD

1   Make the marinade: heat the oil and gently fry the onions and garlic for 2 minutes. Add the remaining marinade ingredients. Leave to cool.

2   Cut the fish into bite-size cubes and place in the marinade with the green pepper. Cover and leave for at least 2 hours.

3   Arrange the marinade fish and peppers on kebab skewers alternating with the prawns, mushrooms, tomatoes and bay leaves.

4   Place on a grill pan and spoon over any remaining marinade.

5   Grill for about 10 minutes each side until the fish is cooked and golden brown.

Salmon in Tomato Sauce

(F 4)

CALORIES: 307

To make this meal less expensive you could try using cod fillets or monkfish instead of the salmon.

PREPARATION TIME: 20 MINUTES
COOKING TIME: 25 MINUTES
TEMPERATURE: 180°C/350°F/GAS 4

INGREDIENTS: IMPERIAL/METRIC
4 salmon steaks
¼pt/150ml fish stock
1 lemon, juice of
1 onion, peeled and sliced
6 peppercorns

SAUCE
1tbsp olive oil
1 bunch spring onions, washed and chopped
1 green pepper, washed, seeded and chopped
8oz/225g tomatoes, washed and quartered
1tbsp dill, chopped   black pepper

METHOD

1   Place the salmon steaks in an ovenproof dish with the fish stock, lemon juice, sliced onion and peppercorns. Cover and bake for 20 minutes until the salmon is cooked.

2   Make the sauce: heat the oil and gently fry the spring onions and green pepper for 2 minutes. Add the tomatoes and heat through.

3   Stir in the dill and season with the black pepper.

4   Spoon the tomato sauce into a serving dish and carefully place the salmon steaks on top. Serve hot.

Salmon Roll

(F 6)

A tasty dish which is beautiful made with salmon but also good with trout or mackerel. The simple ingredient changes have a marked effect on the calorie content but not the taste.

PREPARATION TIME: 30 MINUTES
COOKING TIME: 65 MINUTES
TEMPERATURE: 190°C/375°F/GAS 5

INGREDIENTS: IMPERIAL/METRIC

Traditional Recipe
CALORIES: 868

1lb/450g salmon
4tbsp white wine
6½oz/180g butter
1½oz/40g plain flour
8oz/225g Cheddar cheese, grated
3 eggs, hard-boiled
¼pt/150ml soured cream
2tbsp fresh parsley, chopped
2oz/50g lard
1lb/450g self-raising flour
2 egg yolks
salt and pepper

Swap Shop Recipe
CALORIES: 593

1lb/450g salmon
4tbsp white wine
6½oz/180g polyunsaturated margarine (unhydrogenated)
1½oz/40g wholemeal flour, plain
8oz/225g Gouda cheese, grated
6 asparagus spears, cooked and chopped
¼pt/150ml fromage frais
1 lemon, zest of
2tbsp fresh parsley, chopped
1 recipe low-fat pastry (see page 156)

METHOD

1 Place the salmon in a large saucepan with just enough cold water to cover. Add the wine and simmer for about 20 minutes. Flake the fish, removing all bones and skin. Reserve the cooking liquid.

2 Melt 1½oz/40g of the margarine in a saucepan and stir in the flour. Cook for 1 minute. Remove from the heat and gradually stir in ½pt/275ml of the reserved fish stock. Bring to the boil and simmer for 2 minutes. Remove from the heat and stir in the grated cheese, asparagus, fromage frais, lemon zest and parsley. Leave to cool.

3 Roll out a third of the pastry to an oblong about 12×4in/30×10cm and place on a greased baking sheet. Top with the sauce mixture, salmon and more sauce.

4 Cover with the remaining pastry, sealing the edges well. Decorate with pastry trimmings.

5 Bake for about 40 minutes.

Halibut with Asparagus

(F 4)
CALORIES: 349

The creamy texture and flavour of the asparagus is a perfect match for the halibut. A rich creamy dish which tastes as though it's bad for your health but, of course, isn't.

PREPARATION TIME: 30 MINUTES
COOKING TIME: 25 MINUTES
TEMPERATURE: 180°C/350°F/GAS 4

INGREDIENTS: IMPERIAL/METRIC
4 halibut steaks
8fl oz/220ml white wine or fish stock
1 lemon, juice and zest
6oz/175g button mushrooms, wiped and sliced
1oz/25g polyunsaturated margarine (unhydrogenated)
1oz/25g wholemeal flour, plain
6fl oz/175ml skimmed milk
¼pt/150ml natural low-fat yogurt
12oz/350g asparagus, tinned – drained and chopped
1tbsp parsley, chopped
black pepper

METHOD
1   Season the fish and place in a lightly oiled ovenproof dish. Pour over the wine or stock and half the lemon juice and zest. Cover and poach in a moderate oven for 20 minutes. Keep warm.
2   Sauté the mushrooms in the remaining lemon juice and zest for 2 minutes.
3   Melt the margarine, stir in the flour and cook for

1 minute over a gentle heat. Add the milk and fish juices and bring to the boil for 2 minutes, stirring continuously.

4   Add the yogurt, asparagus, mushrooms and parsley. Season with black pepper.

5   Lift the halibut on to a serving dish and pour the sauce over.

Stuffed Sole

(F 4)
CALORIES: 430

I always think that stuffed dishes look far more interesting with the stuffing inside, not served in a side dish. This recipe is no exception. The contrast between the green spinach and white fish is vivid. It tastes good too!

PREPARATION TIME: 25 MINUTES
COOKING TIME: 35 MINUTES
TEMPERATURE: 180°C/350°F/GAS 4

INGREDIENTS: IMPERIAL/METRIC
1tbsp olive oil
1 onion, peeled and chopped
1½lb/700g spinach, fresh – chopped
1 egg white
black pepper
freshly grated nutmeg
4 lemon sole fillets, skinned and boned
4fl oz/100ml white wine
1 lemon, juiced
1oz/25g polyunsaturated margarine (unhydrogenated)

1oz/25g wholemeal flour, plain
6fl oz/175ml skimmed milk
½tsp English mustard
3oz/75g Edam cheese, grated
2tbsp fromage frais

METHOD

1   Heat the oil and gently fry the onion for 2 minutes,
     then add the spinach. Cook for 3 minutes.

2   Add the egg white, pepper and nutmeg. Cool
     slightly.

3   Divide the spinach mixture between the sole fillets
     and roll each one up from the tail to the head.

4   Place in a lightly greased ovenproof dish and pour
     the wine and lemon juice over the fish. Cover and
     cook for 25 minutes.

5   Melt the margarine, add the flour and stir for 1
     minute over a gentle heat. Add the milk gradually
     and bring to the boil, stirring continuously. Stir in
     the mustard, cheese, juices from cooked fish, black
     pepper and fromage frais. Heat gently. Coat the
     fillets with the sauce and place in the oven,
     uncovered, for a further 5 minutes.

Monkfish in Sauce

(F 4)

Monkfish is underrated. It has a firm texture, which makes it ideal for many dishes, and a lovely flavour which is not overpowered by sauces and herbs.

PREPARATION TIME: 15 MINUTES
COOKING TIME: 10 MINUTES

INGREDIENTS: IMPERIAL/METRIC

Traditional Recipe
CALORIES: 363

1lb/450g monkfish
¼pt/150ml mayonnaise
5tbsp whipping cream
1tbsp lemon juice
1tsp tomato purée
1tbsp capers, chopped
1tbsp gherkins, chopped
salt and pepper

Swap Shop Recipe
CALORIES: 197

1lb/450g monkfish
¼pt/150ml low-fat mayonnaise
5tbsp fromage frais
1tbsp lemon juice
1tsp tomato purée
1tbsp capers, chopped
1tbsp gherkins, chopped
black pepper

METHOD

1   Cut the monkfish into cubes and steam for about 10
    minutes until cooked. Leave to cool.
2   Mix together the low-fat mayonnaise, fromage frais,
    lemon juice, tomato purée, capers, gherkins and
    pepper.
3   Add the monkfish to the sauce and mix well. Divide
    between four plates and serve.

Seafood Pancakes

(F 4)
CALORIES: 247

For a change from prawns and white fish you could try
mussels, shrimp and squid – be adventurous.

PREPARATION TIME: 30 MINUTES
COOKING TIME: 10 MINUTES
TEMPERATURE: 190°C/375°F/GAS 5

INGREDIENTS: IMPERIAL/METRIC
8oz/225g mixed white fish, cooked and cut into bite-size
cubes
8oz/225g prawns, cooked and peeled
1tsp tomato purée
4tbsp fromage frais
olive oil for frying

PANCAKE BATTER
2oz/50g wholemeal flour, plain
2oz/50g white flour, plain
pinch salt
1 egg, beaten
½pt/275ml skimmed milk
1tsp lemon zest

METHOD

1   Put all the pancake batter ingredients into a blender and blend until smooth.

2   Heat a little oil in a frying pan and pour in one tablespoon of the batter and cook until the underneath is golden brown. Carefully turn the pancake over – toss it if you feel brave – and cook for a few seconds.

3   Place the pancake on a warmed plate.

4   Repeat the process with the remaining pancake batter – you should have 12 pancakes. Keep the pancakes warm.

5   Stir the fish, prawns and tomato purée into the fromage frais.

6   Make the pancakes into cone shapes by folding them in half and then in half again.

7   Fill each fold with the fish mixture.

8   Place the pancakes in an ovenproof dish, points downwards, and cook for 10 minutes.

Monkfish and Aubergine Bake

(F 4)
CALORIES: 328

Monkfish and aubergine go really well together and once you add the garlic, tomatoes and cheese you have a very tasty dish on your hands – I guarantee everyone will love it!

PREPARATION TIME: 30 MINUTES
COOKING TIME: 30 MINUTES
TEMPERATURE: 200°C/400°F/GAS 6

INGREDIENTS: IMPERIAL/METRIC
2 aubergines, medium-size
1lb/450g monkfish
4tbsp fresh lemon juice
1tsp lemon zest
2tbsp olive oil
6 spring onions, washed and chopped
3 garlic cloves, crushed
1 green pepper, washed, seeded and chopped
8oz/225g tomatoes, washed and chopped
2tsp fresh basil, chopped
low-sodium salt and black pepper
4oz/125g Edam cheese, grated

METHOD

1 Cut the aubergines in half lengthways. Run a sharp knife around the edge of the flesh and skin and scoop out the flesh. Cut the flesh into bite-size cubes.

2 Sprinkle the aubergine shells and flesh with salt and leave for 30 minutes to draw out the bitter juices.

3 Meanwhile, cut the monkfish into bite-size cubes and season with black pepper. Place in a steamer and sprinkle with the lemon juice and zest. Steam for approximately 10 minutes until cooked.

4 Wash the salt off the aubergines and pat dry with a paper towel.

5 Heat the oil and gently fry the aubergine, onions and garlic until they are almost cooked.

6 Add the green pepper, tomatoes, basil, monkfish and black pepper. Cook for 2 minutes.

7 Pile the mixture into the aubergine shells and top with the grated cheese.

8 Place the aubergine shells in an ovenproof dish and cook for approximately 30 minutes.

Prawn Puffs

(F 4)
CALORIES: 228

Chick peas and prawns are two of my favourite foods and so this combination was inevitable for me. The creamy texture of the filling contrasts beautifully with the crispness of the filo pastry. These little prawn puffs look very attractive garnished with watercress sprigs.

PREPARATION TIME: 25 MINUTES
COOKING TIME: 20 MINUTES
TEMPERATURE: 190°C/375°F/GAS 5

INGREDIENTS: IMPERIAL/METRIC
8oz/225g prawns, cooked and peeled
4oz/125g chick peas, cooked
2tbsp low-fat soft cheese
1tsp tomato purée
black pepper
1 lemon, zest of
8 filo pastry sheets
oil for brushing

METHOD
1 Mix together the first six ingredients.
2 Lightly oil each filo pastry sheet as you use it – this gives it its lovely crispness.
3 Fold each filo sheet in half widthways and place a spoonful of the prawn mixture in the centre. Gather the pastry up and around the filling and twist to close the top. Brush with a little oil and place on a lightly oiled baking sheet.
4 Cook until golden brown, about 20 minutes.

Seafood Lasagne

(F 4)

A lasagne is a very filling dish and a nice salad is really all that is required to accompany it. Any combination of seafood is suitable and when it is coated in this rich but low-fat sauce the taste is superb!

PREPARATION TIME: 15 MINUTES
COOKING TIME: 35 MINUTES
TEMPERATURE: 180°C/350°F/GAS 4

INGREDIENTS: IMPERIAL/METRIC

Traditional Recipe
CALORIES: 724

2tsp corn oil
¾pt/425ml milk
1 onion, peeled and studded with 4 cloves
2 blades mace
4 black peppercorns
1 carrot, peeled and sliced
1 celery stick, washed
2 bay leaves
5oz/150g lasagne
3oz/75g butter
2oz/50g plain flour
1tbsp fresh dill, chopped
4tbsp double cream
7oz/200g tuna, drained and flaked
4oz/125g crab meat, flaked
4oz/125g prawns, cooked
4oz/125g Cheddar cheese, grated

Swap Shop Recipe
CALORIES: 538

2tsp sesame oil
¾pt/425ml skimmed milk
1 onion, peeled and studded with 4 cloves
2 blades mace
4 black peppercorns
1 carrot, scraped and sliced
1 celery stick, washed
2 bay leaves
5oz/150g wholewheat lasagne
2oz/50g polyunsaturated margarine (unhydrogenated)
2oz/50g wholemeal flour, plain
1tbsp fresh dill, chopped
4tbsp fromage frais
7oz/200g tuna in brine,
drained and flaked
4oz/125g crab meat, flaked
4oz/125g prawns, cooked
4oz/125g Edam cheese, grated

METHOD

1 Lightly oil a 3pt/1.7l square dish with 1tsp of the oil.
2 Put the milk into a saucepan with the onion, mace, peppercorns, carrot, celery and bay leaves. Bring to the boil and remove from the heat.
3 Put the remaining oil in a large saucepan of boiling water. Add the lasagne strips and cook for 8 minutes. Drain.
4 Strain the milk. Melt the margarine in a saucepan and stir in the flour. Cook for 1 minute. Remove from the heat and gradually stir in the milk. Bring to the boil, stirring constantly, and cook until the sauce

is smooth and thick. Remove from the heat and stir in the dill, fromage frais, tuna, crab meat and prawns.

5   Pour one third of the sauce into the base of the oiled dish and cover with half the lasagne. Pour on another third of the sauce followed by the remaining lasagne, and then finish with the sauce.

6   Sprinkle with the grated Edam cheese and cook until the top is golden brown – about 35 minutes.

Tandoori Halibut

(F 4)
CALORIES: 258

Tandoori halibut has to be tasted to be believed – definitely one of my favourites.

PREPARATION TIME: 15 MINUTES
+ MARINATING TIME OF 2 HOURS
COOKING TIME: 30 MINUTES
TEMPERATURE: 190°C/375°F/GAS 5

INGREDIENTS: IMPERIAL/METRIC
4 halibut steaks

MARINADE
3 garlic cloves, crushed
4tbsp low-fat natural yogurt
1tbsp sesame seed oil
1tsp ground cumin
½tsp ground coriander
½tsp chilli powder
¼tsp ground turmeric

METHOD

1 Make the marinade by mixing the ingredients together well.
2 Place the halibut steaks in an ovenproof dish and spoon the marinade over. Leave for at least 2 hours.
3 Bake, uncovered, for about 30 minutes until the fish flakes easily.
4 Serve on a bed of boiled brown rice.

Baked Trout

(F 4)
CALORIES: 347

You can't get any simpler than this recipe and it tastes super. I like to eat it with a crispy salad full of fruits. Wonderful!

PREPARATION TIME: 5 MINUTES
COOKING TIME: 30 MINUTES
TEMPERATURE: 180°C/350°F/GAS 4

INGREDIENTS: IMPERIAL/METRIC
4 trout, cleaned, gutted and boned
sprigs of fresh dill, tarragon and rosemary
olive oil
black pepper

METHOD

1 Place a few sprigs of the fresh herbs in the cavity of each trout.
2 Season the trout with the black pepper and brush lightly with the oil.
3 Place in a lightly greased ovenproof dish and bake, uncovered, for about 30 minutes.

Stuffed Mackerel

(F 4)
CALORIES: 578

Fresh mackerel is becoming popular again after being out of favour for a good few years. This recipe looks good and mixes together creamy and crunchy textures. An interesting little number.

PREPARATION TIME: 25 MINUTES
COOKING TIME: 20 MINUTES
TEMPERATURE: MODERATE GRILL

INGREDIENTS: IMPERIAL/METRIC
4 fresh mackerel, cleaned and gutted

STUFFING
2tbsp olive oil
2 garlic cloves, crushed
½ small onion, peeled and finely chopped
4 spring onions, washed and chopped
4oz/125g spinach, chopped finely
4oz/125g watercress, washed and chopped
2oz/50g wholemeal breadcrumbs
1oz/25g Edam cheese, grated
1 tbsp sunflower seeds, toasted
1tsp orange zest
black pepper

METHOD

1 To make the stuffing, heat the oil and gently fry the garlic, onion and spring onions for 2 minutes, stirring occasionally.

2 Add the spinach, watercress, breadcrumbs, cheese, seeds, orange zest and pepper. Stir well.

3   Make diagonal cuts into the flesh of each mackerel.
4   Spoon the stuffing into the fish cavity, pressing firmly, and secure cut edges with cocktail sticks. Place under a moderate grill for 10 minutes each side until the fish flakes.

Cod in Cream and Celery Sauce

(F 4)

A nice combination of flavours and textures in this dish. New potatoes and runner beans are good to serve alongside the fish.

PREPARATION TIME: 20 MINUTES
COOKING TIME: 25 MINUTES
TEMPERATURE: 200°C/400°F/GAS 6

INGREDIENTS: IMPERIAL/METRIC

Traditional Recipe
CALORIES: 464

4 cod steaks
1tbsp lemon juice
2oz/50g butter
3 sticks of celery, trimmed and chopped
1oz/25g flour
8fl oz/225ml milk
4fl oz/125ml double cream
1tsp thyme, chopped
4oz/125g Lancashire cheese, grated
2 tomatoes, sliced
salt and pepper

Swap Shop Recipe
CALORIES: 237

4 cod steaks
1tbsp lemon juice
1tbsp olive oil
3 sticks of celery, trimmed and chopped
1oz/25g wholemeal flour
8fl oz/225ml skimmed milk
4fl oz/125ml fromage frais
black pepper
1tsp thyme, chopped
4oz/125g Gouda cheese, grated
2 tomatoes, sliced

METHOD

1 Sprinkle the fish with lemon juice and season. Place under a moderate grill for about 20 minutes, turning over once, until cooked. Keep warm in an ovenproof dish.

2 Heat the olive oil and fry the celery until tender. Stir in the flour and cook for 1 minute, stirring all the time. Remove the pan from the heat and gradually stir in the milk and fromage frais. Heat until the sauce thickens.

3 Add the black pepper, thyme and 1oz/25g of the cheese.

4 Pour the sauce over the fish and sprinkle with the remaining cheese.

5 Arrange the tomatoes on the sauce and place under a hot grill for 5 minutes to brown.

Mackerel with Orange

(F 4)

CALORIES: 445

The sharpness of the orange complements the flavour of the mackerel without overpowering it. Quick and easy to make – ideal for the busy person.

PREPARATION TIME: 10 MINUTES
COOKING TIME: 20 MINUTES
TEMPERATURE: MODERATELY HIGH GRILL

INGREDIENTS: IMPERIAL/METRIC
4 mackerel, cleaned and gutted
1oz/25g polyunsaturated margarine (unhydrogenated)
1tbsp fresh dill, chopped
1 orange, zest of
black pepper

METHOD

1 Preheat the grill to moderately high.
2 Make diagonal cuts in the flesh of each mackerel.
3 Beat together the margarine, dill, orange zest and pepper.
4 Place the mackerel under the grill and spread half of the margarine mixture over the fish. Grill for 10 minutes.
5 Turn the fish over and repeat the process. Serve hot.

Plaice and Prawn Roulades

(F 4)

CALORIES: 370

A very rich-tasting dish with an array of textures and flavours to set the taste buds on fire.

PREPARATION TIME: 20 MINUTES
COOKING TIME: 25 MINUTES
TEMPERATURE: 190°C/375°F/GAS 5

INGREDIENTS: IMPERIAL/METRIC
1lb/450g whole prawns, cooked and peeled
1tbsp olive oil
6 spring onions, washed and chopped
2 celery sticks, washed and chopped
2tsp lemon zest
black pepper
4 plaice fillets, skinned
¼pt/150ml white wine
3fl oz/75ml fromage frais

METHOD

1   Chop the prawns finely.
2   Heat the oil and add half the spring onions and all the celery. Fry gently for about 1 minute. Add the prawns, lemon zest and black pepper. Remove from the heat.
3   Lay the plaice fillets flat on a work surface and spoon the stuffing over them – press it down quite firmly.
4   Carefully roll up the fillets and place them, join side down, in an ovenproof dish.
5   Pour over the wine, cover and cook for about 25 minutes.

6   Whizz the remaining spring onions in a blender with
the fish juices and fromage frais, then heat the mixture gently in a pan. Serve, seasoned to taste, with
the fish roulades.

Cod Curry

(F 4)
CALORIES: 259

If you have never tasted a fish curry you are in for a real
treat. Monkfish is also good in this recipe.

PREPARATION TIME: 30 MINUTES
COOKING TIME: 30 MINUTES
TEMPERATURE: 190°C/375°F/GAS 5

INGREDIENTS: IMPERIAL/METRIC
1½lb/700g cod fillets, skinned and boned
1tbsp olive oil
1 onion, peeled and chopped
3 garlic cloves, crushed

MARINADE
2tbsp lime juice and zest of the lime
1tsp clear honey
2tsp garam masala
1tsp ground cumin
1tsp ground coriander
½pt/275ml low-fat natural yogurt
1tsp cumin seeds
½tsp turmeric
2tsp grated root ginger
black pepper

METHOD

1 Make the marinade: combine all the ingredients and place in a large glass bowl.
2 Cut the cod into thick slices and place in the marinade. Cover and leave for at least 2 hours.
3 Heat the oil and gently cook the onion and garlic. Place in the bottom of an ovenproof dish.
4 Arrange the cod and marinade over the onion mixture and cover with foil. Cook for about 30 minutes. Serve with brown rice and poppadoms.

Smoked Mackerel Quiche

(F 6)
CALORIES: 312

This quiche is lovely served either hot or cold with a nice green salad.

PREPARATION TIME: 30 MINUTES
COOKING TIME: 50 MINUTES
TEMPERATURE: 180°C/350°F/GAS 4

INGREDIENTS: IMPERIAL/METRIC
1 recipe low-fat pastry (see page 156)

FILLING
1 egg
3 egg whites
½pt/275ml fromage frais
6oz/175g smoked mackerel, skinned, boned and cut into strips
½tsp freshly grated nutmeg
2tsp chopped dill
black pepper

METHOD

1 Line an 8in/20cm flan case with the pastry, prick the base and bake blind for 10 minutes.

2 Beat the egg and egg whites with the fromage frais and add the mackerel, nutmeg, dill and black pepper. Pour into the flan case and cook for 40 minutes until set.

Tuna Moussaka

(F 6)
CALORIES: 452

A simple and substantial meal that needs only a good salad to accompany it.

PREPARATION TIME: 25 MINUTES
COOKING TIME: 1 hour
TEMPERATURE: 190°C/375°F/GAS 5

INGREDIENTS: IMPERIAL/METRIC
3tbsp olive oil
2 aubergines, sliced thinly
1 onion, peeled and sliced
4 garlic cloves, crushed
2tbsp wholemeal flour, plain
½pt/275ml skimmed milk
¼pt/150ml vegetable or fish stock
4oz/125g button mushrooms, wiped and sliced
2×7oz/200g tins tuna fish in brine, drained and flaked
3oz/75g Gouda cheese, grated
1 lemon, zest of
black pepper

TOPPING
½pt/275ml low-fat natural yogurt
4oz/125g low-fat soft cheese

METHOD

1 Brush two baking sheets with a little oil. Arrange the aubergine slices in a single layer on each sheet and brush with oil. Bake for 15 minutes.

2 Heat the remaining oil and gently fry the onion for 3 minutes. Add the garlic and cook for 1 minute.

3 Stir in the flour and cook for 1 minute. Gradually stir in the milk and stock. Bring to the boil and simmer until the sauce thickens, stirring continuously.

4 Add the mushrooms, tuna, cheese, lemon zest and black pepper.

5 Place half the mixture in a lightly greased ovenproof dish and place half the aubergines on top. Add the remaining tuna mixture and use the rest of the aubergines for the final layer.

6 Mix the yogurt and soft cheese together and pour over the moussaka. Bake for about 40 minutes until the top is golden brown.

CHAPTER SEVEN

POULTRY MATTERS

MY ATTITUDE to white meat generally, and chicken in particular, has changed dramatically over the last few months. The reason for this change? Well, to be perfectly honest, it's Dudley Moore! Yes, I do mean the television advertisements where poor old Dud is relentlessly hunting down those very elusive French free-range chickens. I can honestly say that I can't look a chicken in the face without bursting into fits of laughter – not that I look into the faces of chickens that often, you understand!

Chickens and I go back quite a long way. About fifteen years ago I was attending a company dinner and won first prize in the raffle. That's the only time I have won a raffle, and the prize was a large, fresh chicken. Pity I had just become a vegetarian. How's that for Murphy's Law?

Anyway, enough of that, on to more serious matters. The movement towards eating less red meat and more white meat is good for us. The fat content of white meat tends to be lower – except when eaten with the skin on. For example, 100 grams of white meat and skin contains 14 grams of fat, but the same amount of meat without skin contains only 4 grams. Quite a difference – so always cook the birds naked!

So on the whole poultry looks good for our health and our figures. However, although this is true for white meats such as chicken and turkey, it is not true for goose and duck, which are very much fattier and really should be avoided – or eaten in moderation.

All poultry provides a high quality complete protein and is also a good source of the B vitamins and the mineral iron.

POULTRY PRINCIPLES

Buying Guide

Look for a:

- fresh, unblemished skin and clear, unblemished meat;
- a young bird for grilling, roasting or stir-frying as the flesh is more tender than that of older birds which have tougher muscle fibre;
- moist skin that isn't discoloured in any way.

Don't buy self-basting poultry as fat or oil is inserted under the skin of the breast before the bird is packed or frozen. As the bird cooks, the fat warms, melts and bastes the bird. Self-basting birds are higher in fat content and, depending on which oil or fat is used, probably higher in cholesterol.

Cooking Guide

Poultry is quick and easy to cook, and surprisingly difficult to spoil. It is important, however, to keep the following points in mind:

- Always remove the skin before cooking.
- Always place the bird on a trivet when roasting.
- Baste the bird only when absolutely necessary.
- Preheat the oven and ensure the bird is cooked to a uniform temperature of 180°C/350°F. It's the cooking process that kills off the salmonella and other micro-organisms on the skin and flesh.
- Stews and casseroles should always be skimmed to remove excess fat from the surface.

There are many ways to cook poultry and the majority of them are quite healthy. I like my poultry steamed because it makes the flesh beautifully tender – it simply melts in the mouth. Roasting on a trivet, grilling, barbecuing, poaching, stir-frying, etc., are also excellent ways to cook it. Coating poultry pieces in breadcrumbs or batter and then deep-frying them is really to be avoided, but as the other cooking methods are so delicious this shouldn't be too much of a hardship! White meat takes very well to being marinated, which gives it a refreshingly different flavour. Marinating food is so easy and effective that it makes me wonder why we don't do it more often. Now is the time to start.

COMMON PROBLEMS

The main problem people have with poultry is that they associate it with salmonella and whenever there is a scare they stop buying it. Salmonella is a problem but it is easily avoided by ensuring that the poultry is adequately cooked all the way through. This doesn't mean that you cook it until it has the texture and appearance of the famous Hale and Pace rubber chicken. There is a happy medium here! It is better not to stuff the cavity of the bird as this impedes the cooking process somewhat.

You must also ensure that you give all work surfaces, chopping boards, knives, forks, etc. a really good scrub after being in contact with raw poultry to avoid any possibility of cross-contamination. Similarly, when storing raw poultry in the refrigerator make sure it is well wrapped in foil and place it on a plate large enough to catch any drips. By simple measures such as these you will minimize the risk of unpleasant tummy upsets.

Another problem is the way we think of poultry generally. When I think of chicken I still tend to see the standard pub snack popular some years ago – chicken and chips in a basket. Can you remember all those insipid-looking half-cooked legs sitting on a pile of soggy, greasy chips and served, unceremoniously, in a wicker basket with a bright red serviette peeping through the food? Thank goodness it isn't so popular these days. Things have progressed to Malayan chicken and other oriental-type dishes – much more adventurous and, potentially at least, healthier.

Having said this, the British tradition is still to stuff poultry and roast it, which is all very well but it does get a bit boring. You start off with it for dinner on Sunday, have it cold with salad for tea and then have it in sandwiches until it's finished. Christmas is the worst time for that – what on earth do you do with all that surplus meat? Well, there are plenty of ideas in this chapter to keep you going for a good while. And remember, as with anything else, we are only limited by our own imagination.

SWAP SHOP RECIPES

When using chicken as the main ingredient in a recipe, we are starting off with a relatively healthy food. But then we make it unhealthy by what we add to it. It is the oil, fat and creamy rich sauces that pile on the calories, cholesterol and fat content.

Once again, the trick is to substitute the high-fat creams in sauces with low-fat alternatives such as fromage frais, yogurt and tofu. Cook the chicken in such a way as to minimize the fat content and if you do need to use oil make sure it's a healthy one. It's so simple. And, by using herbs and spices for sauces and seasoning, the need to use salt is reduced. The swap shop recipes in this chapter will show you what I mean.

Chinese Chicken

(F 4)
CALORIES: 412

I love Chinese food and this recipe is one of my favour-ites. The vegetables are crisp, the sauce beautifully rich and the ginger adds a nice 'bite' to the whole dish. Try wild rice as a change from brown rice.

PREPARATION TIME: 15 MINUTES
COOKING TIME: 10 MINUTES

INGREDIENTS: IMPERIAL/METRIC
2tbsp olive oil
2 garlic cloves, crushed
1 onion, peeled and sliced
1 red pepper, seeded and cut into strips
4oz/125g button mushrooms, wiped and halved
4oz/125g brown rice (uncooked weight), cooked
1lb/450g cooked chicken meat, skinned
and cut into strips
6 canned water chestnuts, sliced
2tbsp bamboo shoots
8oz/225g bean sprouts
2tsp cornflour
1tbsp soy sauce
¼pt/150ml chicken stock
1tbsp sake or dry sherry
1 bunch spring onions, washed and chopped
4 pieces stem ginger, chopped

METHOD

1 Heat the oil in a large frying pan. Add the garlic, onion, red pepper and mushrooms. Cook for 2 minutes, stirring occasionally.
2 Add the rice, chicken, water chestnuts, bamboo shoots and bean sprouts and cook for 3 minutes.
3 Stir the cornflour into the soy sauce and mix with the chicken stock and sake or sherry. Add to the pan and bring to the boil, stirring continuously. Simmer for 3 minutes.
4 Stir in the spring onions and ginger and serve.

Stuffed Vine Leaves

(F 4)
CALORIES: 296

You can use spinach, spring cabbage or lettuce leaves if you can't find vine leaves. I always think that 'parcelled' food looks very attractive and yet is deceptively easy to prepare. The texture of this dish is rough, which I like.

PREPARATION TIME: 15 MINUTES
COOKING TIME: 40 MINUTES
TEMPERATURE: 190°C/375°F/GAS 5

INGREDIENTS: IMPERIAL/METRIC
8oz/225g pkt vine leaves, drained and rinsed
1tbsp olive oil
1 onion, peeled and chopped very finely
8oz/225g chicken meat, raw and minced
2oz/50g wholemeal breadcrumbs

2oz/50g sunflower seeds
1 lemon, zest and juice
1 tsp sage
black pepper
7fl oz/200ml chicken stock

METHOD

1 Separate the vine leaves, and put them in a large bowl. Cover them with boiling water and leave to soak.

2 Heat the oil in a saucepan and fry the onion for 2 minutes. Add the chicken and cook for 3 minutes.

3 Stir in the breadcrumbs, sunflower seeds, lemon zest and juice, sage and pepper. Stir well.

4 Drain the vine leaves and remove the stems. Lay each leaf shiny-side down on a flat work surface and place about 1 tablespoon of the chicken mixture in the centre. Fold the leaf over to cover the filling completely. Combine 2 or 3 leaves if they are especially small before adding the stuffing.

5 Place the stuffed leaves in a shallow ovenproof dish, packed tightly together, pour the stock over and cover with foil. Cook for 35 minutes.

Turkey Cobbler

(F 6)

A very filling meal this one! The rich-tasting scone-type topping complements the creamy turkey mixture well – I love it.

PREPARATION TIME: 30 MINUTES
COOKING TIME: 45 MINUTES
TEMPERATURE: 220°C/425°F/GAS 7

INGREDIENTS: IMPERIAL/METRIC

Traditional Recipe
CALORIES: 598

2 turkey joints
2oz/50g butter
4oz/125g mushrooms, sliced
½pt/275ml milk
¼pt/150ml cream
1 chicken stock cube
1tsp lemon juice
9oz/250g plain flour
2tsp baking powder
3oz/75g butter

Swap Shop Recipe
CALORIES: 516

2 turkey joints, skinned
1tbsp olive oil
4oz/125g mushrooms, sliced
½pt/275ml skimmed milk
¾pt/150ml chicken stock
1tsp lemon juice
5oz/150g wholemeal flour, plain
4oz/100g white flour, plain
3tsp low-sodium baking powder
3oz/75g polyunsaturated margarine (unhydrogenated)

METHOD

1 Cut each turkey joint in half. Heat the oil and fry the turkey and mushrooms for about 5 minutes. Remove the mushrooms.

2 Add the milk, chicken stock and lemon juice to the turkey. Bring to the boil, cover and simmer for 30 minutes.

3 Mix 1oz/25g flour to a smooth paste with a little water.

4 Remove the turkey from the pan and cut the flesh from the bones. Return the flesh to the pan with the flour paste and stir well. Bring to the boil and stir until thickened. Add the mushrooms.

5 Make the scone topping by sifting together the remaining flour and the baking powder. Rub in the margarine until the mixture resembles fine bread-crumbs. Add enough water to make a soft dough. Press out on a floured work surface to about ½in/1cm thick and shape to the size of the dish.

6 Place the turkey mixture in an ovenproof dish with the scone mixture on the top. Brush with a little milk and bake in the oven for about 15 minutes until the top is a lovely golden colour.

Mexican Chicken

(F 4–6)

CALORIES: 372

I would describe this dish as pleasantly hot. You may need to increase or decrease the amount of chilli to suit your taste buds – you'll get it right by trial and error!

PREPARATION TIME: 5 MINUTES
COOKING TIME: 45 MINUTES
TEMPERATURE: 190°C/375°F/GAS 5

INGREDIENTS: IMPERIAL/METRIC
1lb/450g chicken meat, raw and cut into strips
1tbsp wholemeal flour, plain
1tbsp olive oil
1 onion, peeled and sliced
2 garlic cloves, crushed
1tsp chilli powder
1 red chilli, seeded and chopped finely
1 green chilli, seeded and chopped finely
black pepper
1 × 8oz/225g tin tomatoes, with juices
1 × 15oz/425g tin red kidney beans, drained

METHOD

1   Toss the chicken meat in the wholemeal flour.
2   Heat the oil in a frying pan and fry the chicken for 5 minutes until it is lightly browned. Remove from the pan.
3   Place the onions in the frying pan with the garlic and cook for 2 minutes before adding the chilli powder, chillies and black pepper. Cook for 2 minutes.
4   Add the tomatoes and kidney beans and simmer for 5 minutes. Add the chicken and stir well.
5   Pour the mixture into a casserole dish, cover, and cook for about 30 minutes.

Steamed Chicken Breasts

(F 4)
CALORIES: 219

You cannot fail with steamed chicken breasts – guaranteed to be tender and flavoursome. The peanut butter gives the dish a nice nutty flavour and texture.

PREPARATION TIME: 5 MINUTES
COOKING TIME: 20 MINUTES

INGREDIENTS: IMPERIAL/METRIC
4 chicken breasts, skinned and boned
3tbsp breadcrumbs, wholemeal
2oz/50g Edam or Gouda cheese, grated
2tsp peanut butter, crunchy
black pepper

METHOD
1 Create two pockets in each chicken breast by making two deep cuts in the flesh.
2 Mix together the breadcrumbs, cheese, peanut butter and black pepper.
3 Stuff the mixture into the chicken breasts and steam for about 20 minutes until the meat is tender.

Turkey and Orange Casserole

(F 4)
CALORIES: 326

Now, turkey and orange may seem an unusual combination but it does work – just try it and see!

PREPARATION TIME: 5 MINUTES
COOKING TIME: 1 HOUR 10 MINUTES

INGREDIENTS: IMPERIAL/METRIC
2tbsp olive oil
1 onion, peeled and chopped
1 orange, zest and juice
2tsp fresh sage, chopped
12oz/350g turkey, boned and cut into cubes
black pepper
1tbsp wholemeal flour, plain
¼pt/150ml chicken stock
¼pt/150ml Norfolk Punch* or chicken stock
6 juniper berries, crushed

METHOD

1   Heat the oil in an ovenproof casserole dish and
    gently fry the onion for about 2 minutes. Add the
    orange zest and sage and fry for 1 minute.
2   Toss the turkey cubes in the flour, seasoned with the
    black pepper, and add to the casserole. Fry for 3
    minutes, stirring occasionally.
3   Gradually stir in the orange juice, stock, Norfolk
    Punch, and juniper berries. Cover and simmer for
    about 1 hour. Serve hot.

*Norfolk Punch is available from healthfood shops.

Chicken and Broccoli Loaf

(F 4)
CALORIES: 275

Another one of my favourite dishes. In slices, the white
of the chicken contrasts with the green of the broccoli

and looks stunning. Try using different vegetables for the central stripe when you want a change.

PREPARATION TIME: 25 MINUTES
COOKING TIME: 1 HOUR 30 MINUTES
TEMPERATURE: 180°C/350°F/GAS 4

INGREDIENTS: IMPERIAL/METRIC
1lb/450g chicken meat, raw and minced
3oz/75g button mushrooms, wiped and sliced
1 onion, peeled and chopped
2oz/50g wholemeal breadcrumbs
2 egg whites, beaten
2tbsp Greek strained yogurt
½tsp tarragon
black pepper
4oz/125g broccoli spears, lightly steamed

METHOD

1 Mix together the chicken, mushrooms, onion, breadcrumbs, egg whites, yogurt, tarragon and black pepper.

2 Grease and line a 1lb/450g loaf tin, place half the chicken mixture in the bottom and press down firmly.

3 Make the next layer with the broccoli spears and then top with the remaining chicken mixture. Press down firmly.

4 Cover with foil and place in a roasting tin half filled with boiling water.

5 Bake for about 1 hour 30 minutes. Serve either hot or cold.

Turkey Breasts with Chestnuts

(F 4)
CALORIES: 621

I concocted this recipe for Christmas dinner one year to make a change from the traditional turkey dinner. Everyone enjoyed their meal and the chestnut flavour made all the difference – it even made it more Christmassy!

PREPARATION TIME: 25 MINUTES
COOKING TIME: 30 MINUTES

INGREDIENTS: IMPERIAL/METRIC
2tbsp olive oil
1lb/450g turkey breasts, skinned and sliced
2 onions, peeled and chopped
1 red pepper, seeded and chopped
1tbsp wholemeal flour, plain
½pt/275ml chicken stock
¼pt/150ml white wine, dry
1tsp tarragon
1lb/450g whole chestnuts, tinned and drained
4tbsp Greek strained yogurt
black pepper

METHOD
1   Heat the oil and fry the turkey breasts for 2 minutes each side. Remove from the pan.
2   Add the onions and red pepper to the pan and fry gently for about 3 minutes.
3   Sprinkle in the flour and cook, stirring continuously, for 1 minute. Gradually add the stock and wine, stirring continuously. Add the tarragon and chestnuts.

4   Return the turkey to the pan and cook gently for 20 minutes. Remove and place on a serving dish. Keep warm.
5   Add the yogurt to the pan with the black pepper and stir gently. Pour the sauce over the turkey and serve hot.

Chicken Mille Feuille

(F 4)

An impressive, yet easy, recipe which is perfect for a dinner party. Using filo pastry gives the same effect as rough puff pastry but with only a fraction of the fat and calories.

PREPARATION TIME: 20 MINUTES
COOKING TIME: 30 MINUTES
TEMPERATURE: 200°C/400°F/GAS 6

INGREDIENTS: IMPERIAL/METRIC

Traditional Recipe
CALORIES: 991

12oz/350g rough puff pastry
2oz/50g butter
2oz/50g plain flour
¾pt/425ml milk
¼pt/150ml cream
8oz/225g button mushrooms, sliced
1 lemon, juiced
1tsp tarragon, dried
12oz/350g chicken, cooked and diced
3oz/75g Cheddar cheese, grated
salt and pepper

Swap Shop Recipe
CALORIES: 557

5 sheets filo pastry
1tsp sesame oil
2oz/50g polyunsaturated margarine (unhydrogenated)
2oz/50g wholemeal flour, plain
¾pt/425ml skimmed milk
¼pt/150ml fromage frais
black pepper
8oz/225g button mushrooms, sliced
1 lemon, juiced
1tsp tarragon, dried
12oz/350g chicken, cooked and diced
3oz/75g Edam cheese, grated

METHOD

1   Cut the filo pastry into 15 strips of approximately 12×4in/30×10cm. Lightly oil each strip. Place five of the strips on top of each other on a greased baking tray; repeat with the remaining pastry so that you have three sets of five strips. Bake for 15 minutes until crisp and golden. Leave to one side.

2   Melt the margarine in a small saucepan, stir in the flour and cook for 1 minute. Remove from the heat and gradually stir in the milk and bring to the boil, stirring continuously. Simmer for about 2 minutes until smooth and thick. Stir in the fromage frais and remove from the heat. Season with black pepper.

3   Sauté the mushrooms quickly in the lemon juice with the tarragon.

4   Mix together the sauce, chicken and mushroom mixture.

5   Spread half the chicken mixture on one set of filo

pastry strips in an ovenproof dish or large plate. Cover with another set of pastry strips and chicken mixture and lay the final pastry on top. Sprinkle with the cheese and bake for about 10 minutes.

Chicken with Mustard

(F 4)

CALORIES: 462

I don't like mustard too much unless it is used sparingly to enhance rather than overpower flavours. In this dish the combination of wholegrain mustard, chicken and courgettes works particularly well.

PREPARATION TIME: 25 MINUTES
COOKING TIME: 1 HOUR 15 MINUTES

INGREDIENTS: IMPERIAL/METRIC
2tbsp olive oil
2 carrots, scraped and sliced
1 onion, peeled and sliced
1 leek, washed and sliced
8oz/225g courgettes, washed and sliced
4 chicken pieces
1tbsp wholemeal flour, plain
1pt/550ml chicken stock
2tbsp wholegrain mustard
¼pt/150ml low-fat natural yogurt

METHOD
1   Heat the oil and fry the carrots, onion, leek and courgettes for about 5 minutes.
2   Toss the chicken pieces in the flour and add to the

onion mixture. Cook for 5 minutes, stirring occasionally.

3   Stir in any remaining flour, the stock and the mustard. Bring to the boil and simmer for 1 hour in a covered pan.

4   Remove the chicken and vegetables from the pan and keep warm in a serving dish.

5   Simmer the liquid until it is reduced by half. Stir occasionally. Remove from the heat and stir in the yogurt. Heat gently.

6   Pour the sauce over the chicken and serve.

Turkey Kebabs

(F 4)
CALORIES: 407

Kebabs are a fun food – children especially like them. Any type of vegetables and fruit can be used to vary the appearance, taste and texture of the kebab. Mango cubes, although unusual, taste great!

**PREPARATION TIME: 15 MINUTES
+ MARINATING TIME OF 5 HOURS
COOKING TIME: 20 MINUTES**

INGREDIENTS: IMPERIAL/METRIC
1lb/450g turkey meat, boned, skinned and cut into bite-size pieces
8oz/225g button mushrooms, wiped
4oz/125g courgettes, washed and sliced very thickly
1 orange, peeled and segmented
1 banana, peeled and sliced very thickly

MARINADE
4fl oz/125ml white wine, dry
1tbsp olive oil
3tbsp lemon or lime juice and zest
3 garlic cloves, crushed
fresh rosemary, chopped
black pepper

METHOD

1   Mix together marinade ingredients and pour over the turkey. Leave in a cool place for at least 5 hours, stirring occasionally.

2   Thread the turkey pieces, mushrooms, courgettes, orange segments and banana on to 4 long skewers and place under a hot grill.

3   Grill the kebabs for 15–20 minutes, basting frequently with the marinade, and turn once during cooking. Serve hot.

Turkey Rolls

(F 4)
CALORIES: 251

Yes, I know the addition of redcurrants, apricots and apples does sound a little over the top but the combination of flavours works surprisingly well. These turkey rolls are lovely and moist – and they look wonderful too.

PREPARATION TIME: 45 MINUTES
COOKING TIME: 45 MINUTES
TEMPERATURE: 190°C/375°F/GAS 5

INGREDIENTS: IMPERIAL/METRIC
4 turkey fillets
½ onion, peeled and chopped
1oz/25g brown rice, cooked
2oz/50g redcurrants
4oz/125g apricots, chopped
4oz/125g dessert apple, chopped
1 lemon, zest of
2tsp basil
black pepper
4 lettuce leaves, washed
1 orange, zest and juice
1tsp apricot jam, no added sugar

METHOD

1 Using a mallet or rolling pin, pound the turkey fillets until they are quite thin.

2 Mix together the onion, brown rice, redcurrants, apricots, apple, lemon zest, basil and black pepper.

3 Place a lettuce leaf on top of each turkey fillet and spoon on the onion mixture. Do not overfill.

4 Roll up the turkey fillets swiss-roll style and secure with either string or a wooden cocktail stick.

5 Place the rolls in an ovenproof dish with the orange juice and cover tightly. Bake for about 45 minutes until the meat is cooked.

6 Pour the juices into a saucepan and stir in the apricot jam and the orange zest. Bring to the boil and boil vigorously for about 3 minutes.

7 Remove the string or cocktail sticks from the turkey rolls and place them on a warm serving plate. Pour the sauce over and serve.

Chicken Breasts with Peppers

(F 4)
CALORIES: 373

Delicious, absolutely delicious!

PREPARATION TIME: 30 MINUTES
COOKING TIME: 40 MINUTES
TEMPERATURE: 200°C/400°F/GAS 6

INGREDIENTS: IMPERIAL/METRIC
4 chicken breasts, skinned and boned
2tbsp olive oil
½ orange pepper, seeded and finely chopped
½ red pepper, seeded and finely chopped
4 spring onions, washed and chopped
1tbsp sunflower seeds
4 garlic cloves, crushed
½ stick celery, washed and finely chopped
4tbsp wholemeal breadcrumbs
4 pieces stem ginger, chopped
2oz/50g Edam cheese, grated
2oz/50g Roule light (garlic and herb soft cheese)
black pepper

METHOD
1 With a sharp knife, make 2 deep slits in the chicken
  breasts – as if you are slicing a teacake almost in half
  to make a sandwich.
2 Heat the oil and fry the peppers, spring onions,
  sunflower seeds, garlic and celery for 2 minutes. Mix
  in the remaining ingredients.
3 Stuff each chicken breast with the pepper mixture
  and place in an ovenproof dish. Cover with foil and

bake for about 35 minutes until the chicken is tender.

Turkey Stroganoff

(F 4)
CALORIES: 451

Using tofu instead of the usual cream cuts right down on the calories without changing the rich nature of the dish. Brown or wild rice complements this stroganoff very well.

PREPARATION TIME: 20 MINUTES
COOKING TIME: 20 MINUTES

INGREDIENTS: IMPERIAL/METRIC
1lb/450g turkey fillet
2tbsp olive oil
1 onion, peeled and finely sliced
3 garlic cloves, crushed
2tbsp chicken stock
nutmeg, freshly grated
low-sodium salt
black pepper
8oz/225g button mushrooms, wiped and sliced
1 green pepper, seeded and finely sliced
4tbsp silken tofu, liquidized

METHOD
1　Thinly slice the turkey.
2　Heat the oil and brown the turkey strips. Add the onion and garlic and fry gently for a few minutes. Add the stock.

3   Season with nutmeg and salt and pepper. Cover the
    pan and simmer for 5 minutes until the turkey is just
    tender.
4   Add the mushrooms and pepper and cook for a
    further 5 minutes. Stir occasionally.
5   Reduce the heat and stir in the tofu. Serve hot.

Coronation Chicken

(F 6)

A traditional dish which is very easily converted into a
much healthier version while the look and taste remain
virtually the same.

PREPARATION TIME: 25 MINUTES
COOKING TIME: 20 MINUTES

INGREDIENTS: IMPERIAL/METRIC

Traditional Recipe
CALORIES: 828

5lb/2.3kg chicken, cooked
2oz/50g butter
1 onion, peeled and sliced
2tbsp curry paste
1tbsp tomato purée
4fl oz/125ml red wine
1 bay leaf
4 tinned apricots, chopped
½pt/275ml mayonnaise
¼pt/150ml double cream
salt and pepper

Swap Shop Recipe
CALORIES: 661

5lb/2.3 kg chicken, skinned and cooked
1tbsp olive oil
1 onion, peeled and sliced
1tbsp curry paste
1tbsp tomato purée
4fl oz/125ml red wine
1 lemon, juiced
1 bay leaf
4 dried apricots, soaked and chopped
½pt/275ml low-fat mayonnaise
¼pt/150ml fromage frais
black pepper

METHOD

1 Remove all the flesh from the chicken and cut into bite-size pieces.

2 Heat the oil in a small saucepan and cook the onion for 2 minutes. Add the curry paste, tomato purée, wine, some of the lemon juice and the bay leaf.

3 Simmer, uncovered, for 10 minutes. Strain and leave to cool.

4 Place the apricots in a food processor with a little of the mayonnaise and blend into a purée. Mix with the remaining mayonnaise and the onion mixture.

5 Fold the fromage frais into the mixture and season with the pepper. Taste and add a little more lemon juice if required.

6 Toss the chicken pieces into the sauce and heat thoroughly before serving.

Chicken Roulades

(F 4)

CALORIES: 353

Garlic and soft cheese are naturals together and when you add the chicken you are on to a winner!

PREPARATION TIME: 30 MINUTES
COOKING TIME: 45 MINUTES

INGREDIENTS: IMPERIAL/METRIC
4oz/125g Roule light (garlic and herb soft cheese)
2 garlic cloves, crushed
4 chicken breasts, skinned and boned
1tbsp olive oil
¼pt/150ml red wine
½pt/275ml chicken stock
1tsp arrowroot
low-sodium salt
black pepper

METHOD

1   Beat the Roule until it is smooth. Add the garlic.
2   Beat out the chicken breasts until they are fairly flat.
3   Spread the cheese mixture evenly on one side of each chicken breast. Roll up the breasts and secure with wooden cocktail sticks.
4   Heat the oil and brown the chicken rolls. Pour in the red wine and chicken stock. Season.
5   Bring to the boil, cover and simmer for 40 minutes. Remove the cocktail sticks, place the chicken in a serving dish and keep warm.
6   Blend the arrowroot with a little water until smooth and pour into the red wine mixture. Heat and stir

until the mixture thickens. Season to taste and spoon over the chicken. Serve piping hot.

Chicken with Cider

(F 4)
CALORIES: 470

Adding cider to this dish gives a nice flavour to the chicken. You could use white wine if you prefer but I like the apple flavour of the cider – especially with the cheese.

PREPARATION TIME: 20 MINUTES
COOKING TIME: 1 HOUR 25 MINUTES
TEMPERATURE: 160°C/325°F/GAS 3

INGREDIENTS: IMPERIAL/METRIC
4 chicken breasts, skinned
2oz/50g polyunsaturated margarine (unhydrogenated)
1oz/25g wholemeal flour
½tsp mustard powder
½pt/275ml skimmed milk
½pt/275ml dry cider
4oz/125g Edam cheese, grated
black pepper

METHOD
1   Place the chicken breasts in a flameproof dish with half the margarine. Bake for about 1¼ hours.
2   Melt the remaining margarine and stir in the flour and mustard. Cook gently for 1 minute, stirring continuously.
3   Remove the pan from the heat and gradually stir in

the milk and cider. Bring to the boil and cook until the sauce thickens, stirring continuously. Simmer for a few minutes.
4 Remove from the heat and stir in 3oz/75g of the cheese and season with the black pepper.
5 Pour the cider-and-cheese sauce over the chicken and sprinkle with the remaining cheese.
6 Place under a hot grill until brown.

Chicken Julienne

(F 4)

A wonderfully colourful dish with the green mangetout and parsley and the red pepper mingling seductively with the white chicken.

PREPARATION TIME: 20 MINUTES
COOKING TIME: 25 MINUTES

INGREDIENTS: IMPERIAL/METRIC
6oz/175g brown rice
1½oz/40g polyunsaturated margarine (unhydrogenated)
1½oz/40g wholemeal flour
½pt/275ml skimmed milk
½pt/275ml chicken stock
12oz/350g cooked chicken, cut into long narrow strips
2tbsp lemon juice
4oz/125g mangetout, washed and topped
4oz/125g red pepper, washed, seeded and cut
into long thin narrow strips
black pepper
1tbsp parsley, chopped

METHOD

1 Cook the rice in plenty of boiling, slightly salted water until it is just tender but not soft. Drain and keep hot.

2 Melt the margarine in a pan, stir in the flour and cook gently for 1 minute, stirring continuously.

3 Remove the pan from the heat and gradually stir in the milk and stock. Bring to the boil and cook until the sauce thickens.

4 Gently stir in the chicken, lemon juice, mangetout, red pepper and black pepper. Heat through for about 10 minutes.

5 Add the parsley to the cooked rice and toss lightly. Arrange the rice on a serving plate and pour the chicken mixture into the centre. Serve immediately.

Chicken Curry

(F 4)
CALORIES: 340

The one thing that deters me from making curries too often is the long list of ingredients. What a daunting prospect, I always think. But this recipe is worth the effort – it is delicious.

PREPARATION TIME: 30 MINUTES
COOKING TIME: 35 MINUTES

INGREDIENTS: IMPERIAL/METRIC
1tbsp olive oil
3 onions, peeled and thinly sliced
2tsp cumin seeds
2tsp ground cumin

2tsp ground coriander
2tsp garam masala
1lb/450g cauliflower florets
8oz/225g carrots, scraped and sliced
8oz/225g courgettes, washed and sliced
1 red pepper, seeded and chopped
1lb/450g chicken, cooked and chopped
¼pt/150ml skimmed milk
1 mango, peeled and chopped
black pepper

METHOD

1 Heat the oil and gently fry the onion and cumin seeds for about 3 minutes. Add the ground cumin, coriander and garam masala and cook for a further 2 minutes.
2 Add the rest of the vegetables, the chicken and the milk.
3 Simmer for about 30 minutes.
4 Add the mango and season with the black pepper. Serve with brown rice.

Stuffed Chicken

(F 6)
CALORIES: 548

Boning a chicken is not easy but the effort is worthwhile: when you slice this chicken, the effect is stunning. (In this recipe we are, for once, leaving the skin on as a special treat!)

PREPARATION TIME: 45 MINUTES
COOKING TIME: 1 HOUR 35 MINUTES
TEMPERATURE: 190°C/375°F/GAS 5

INGREDIENTS: IMPERIAL/METRIC
3½lb/1.5kg roasting chicken
¼pt/150ml chicken stock
3tbsp Norfolk Punch* or sherry

STUFFING
1 tbsp olive oil
1 onion, peeled and chopped finely
8oz/225g button mushrooms, wiped and thinly sliced
3tbsp wholemeal breadcrumbs
2tsp rosemary, chopped
1tsp tarragon, chopped
1 lemon, zest and juice
1 egg white, beaten
black pepper

METHOD
1   Bone the chicken, taking care not to puncture the skin. Spread out the chicken, skin-side downwards, and season.
2   Make the stuffing: heat the oil and gently fry the onion for 2 minutes. Add the mushrooms and fry for

1 minute. Cool slightly. Combine with the bread-crumbs, herbs and lemon zest. Bind together with the egg white and lemon juice. Season.

3 Spread the stuffing mixture over the chicken and sew up.

4 Place in a roasting tin with the stock and Norfolk Punch* or sherry and bake for 1½ hours, basting occasionally. Serve either hot or cold.

*Norfolk Punch is available from healthfood shops.

CHAPTER EIGHT

LIFE AFTER MEAT
AND TWO VEG

To MANY people a vegetarian meal would, at best, consist of an omelette with chips or a cheese salad. These are the two alternatives I always seem to have when we eat in a pub. And neither of these is particularly good for your health. So often a healthy vegetarian meal is thought to be tasteless, boring and unappetizing. I wish I had collected a pound coin for each time these words have been spoken to me at the very suggestion of vegetarian cuisine. In some cases, I must admit, these phrases may be well justified.

Last year we had an Australian couple staying at our guest house – a lovely couple in their late fifties. Upon being asked whether they preferred vegetarian or traditional cuisine the husband very eagerly stressed traditional food, causing a frown to appear on his wife's face. Traditional cuisine was considered a treat for him as he had heart trouble and was vegetarian at home for medical reasons. I expressed great surprise at his change in eating habits when abroad. But more surprising was the explanation for this change. Not being a cook himself he unwillingly ate what his wife considered to be vegetarian cuisine – a plate of cooked vegetables served with boiled potatoes! We soon showed them there was more to vegetarian food than that! They left us to return to Australia with a good selection of my recipes and a whole new outlook on vegetarian cuisine.

The basis of traditional main course meals is either red meat, poultry or fish and these are easy to replace with pulses, legumes, grains, seeds and vegetables. There is no point, from the health angle, in replacing the high-fat meats in a recipe with other high-fat ingredients such as cheese and eggs. This defeats the object. So being vegetarian is not synonymous with eating a healthy diet as many people believe. My recipes rely heavily on low-fat ingredients, but that does not mean the meals are short on taste.

The main course is the centrepiece of any meal and it is well worth a little extra effort to present it with style and imagination. The appearance of a dish makes such a difference. Just spend a few minutes trying to imagine what the meal will look like on the plate, thinking particularly of colours, textures and shapes. Arrange the food on the plate rather than simply spooning piles of it anywhere. It only takes a minute and yet it makes such a big difference to the appearance of the meal and, as a result, makes it more appetizing. Vegetarian food is colourful and exciting and this should be reflected in its presentation.

COMMON PROBLEMS

The main problem people seem to encounter is what to serve! There is much more to vegetarian cuisine than simply knocking the meat off the plate. Cooking healthily involves thinking about food in a different way. The method of cooking and the ingredients used need to be reassessed. Initially it may be difficult to imagine a main course without meat, but once you realize that vegetables need not be relegated to being a mere accompaniment to meat an exciting new concept in food opens up. The recipes in this chapter will give you some idea of the variety and scope available and, hopefully, give you ideas to try for yourself.

The time element seems to be another problem for many people – or, rather, they think it is. Initially you may find that cooking vegetarian takes a little longer than cooking traditional. However, in most cases, this is because you are attempting something new which involves quite a bit of thought and not because it is vegetarian. It is not just a case of switching into automatic pilot any more for choosing your ingredients and cooking them – you now have to concentrate and this takes both time and effort. Once you become familiar with the processes involved you will find that it takes no longer to cook vegetarian – in fact it can be much quicker. For one thing there is no meat to contend with, and that accounts for a large slice of the cooking time of a dish. Fresh vegetables, fruit, pulses and legumes are used instead. And although soaking is required for some legumes, such as dried beans, this only takes a minute to prepare, and pulses, such as lentils, need no soaking at all. If you're in a hurry then tinned legumes are available which are quite good but most contain added salt – read the labels. The use of a pressure cooker will also cut down the cooking time involved.

People often tell me that when they have tried to cook a vegetarian meal the result is bland and tasteless. One of the main causes is overcooking the vegetables which makes them lose most of their flavour, not to mention their texture. Another cause, particularly if salt is not used, is the seasoning. Herbs and spices are an important part of any cooking but they are of paramount importance in vegetarian cuisine. Experiment with the many herbs and spices available and you will soon see that no dish need be tasteless.

SWAP SHOP RECIPES

Transforming traditional main course meals into healthy ones is very easy once you know some of the ground rules. The thing to remember is that we are aiming to reduce the amount of salt, sugar and fat, particularly saturated fat, in our diet and to increase the amount of fibre. Translating this information into everyday eating habits means that meat is replaced with pulses, legumes, grains and vegetables and that high-fat dairy products are replaced with low-fat alternatives. This not only cuts down on fat intake but also increases fibre intake. The amount of salt used in cooking and at the table can be reduced, even eliminated, by seasoning with herbs, spices and fruit zests (scrub the fruit well before you zest it). It is surprising how quickly your taste buds will adapt to eating less salt.

If you feel that you cannot make these changes all at once then do it gradually, perhaps reducing the meat content in a recipe by half and using lentils instead. It is far better to do this than not to make any change to your diet at all. You will probably find that as you become accustomed to eating less meat you will actually prefer eating healthy vegetarian meals.

Low-Fat Pastry

(F V)
CALORIES: 229

This pastry cuts down on the need for fat by using yeast to 'lighten' it. The addition of the yeast also makes the pastry easier to handle than the 'normal' wholemeal variety.

PREPARATION TIME: 25 MINUTES

INGREDIENTS: IMPERIAL/METRIC
5oz/150g plain wholemeal flour
1oz/25g soya flour
½tsp dried yeast, easy blend
pinch of vitamin C powder
1 egg white, lightly beaten
1fl oz/25ml sesame oil, cold pressed
6tsp warm water

METHOD

1 Mix the flours, yeast and vitamin C in a bowl and add the egg white.

2 Mix the oil and warm water together and add to the bowl.

3 Form the dough into a ball and knead on a lightly floured work surface for about 6 or 7 minutes.

4 Leave the dough to rest in a lightly oiled polythene bag until required.

French Onion Tart

(F V 6)

PREPARATION TIME: 25 MINUTES
COOKING TIME: 60 MINUTES
TEMPERATURE: 200°C/400°F/GAS 6

INGREDIENTS: IMPERIAL/METRIC

Traditional Recipe
CALORIES: 353

8oz/225g shortcrust pastry
2oz/50g butter
1lb/450g onions, peeled and sliced
1tsp salt
2 eggs
3fl oz/75ml cream
3oz/75g Cheddar cheese, grated

Swap Shop Recipe
CALORIES: 205

1 recipe low-fat pastry (see opposite)
2tbsp olive oil
1lb/450g onions, peeled and sliced
½tsp tarragon
2 egg whites, beaten
3fl oz/75ml silken tofu, liquidized
3oz/75g low-fat vegetarian cheese, grated

METHOD

1 Make pastry as directed and line a 10in/25cm flan case. Prick the base with a fork and bake blind for 15 minutes.

2　Heat the olive oil in a large saucepan and fry the onion until soft – about 2 minutes.

3　Mix together the remaining ingredients and stir in the onions. Pour the mixture into the flan case.

4　Bake until the flan is firm to the touch – about 40 minutes. Serve either hot or cold.

Spiced Parcels

(F V 8)
CALORIES: 143

These delicious, fragrantly spiced parcels are equally good eaten hot or cold – especially with some garlic and tofu dip (page 66).

PREPARATION TIME: 40 MINUTES
COOKING TIME: 30 MINUTES
TEMPERATURE: 200°C/400°F/GAS 6

INGREDIENTS: IMPERIAL/METRIC
2tbsp extra virgin olive oil
2tsp cumin seeds
1tsp garam masala
1tsp ground coriander
4oz/125g potatoes, washed and diced
4oz/125g onion, peeled and diced
2 garlic cloves, peeled and crushed
4oz/125g spinach, washed
4oz/125g chick peas, washed, soaked and cooked
1tbsp tahini
black pepper
1 recipe low-fat pastry (see page 156)

METHOD

1 Heat the oil in a medium-sized saucepan and add the cumin seeds and spices. Cook for 2 minutes.

2 Add the diced potato, onion and garlic and gently cook for about 10 minutes.

3 Add the spinach and cook for 4 minutes.

4 Add the chick peas, tahini and pepper. Cook for 2 minutes, stirring.

5 Roll out the pastry into a rectangle measuring 12×24in/30×60cm and divide into eight 6in/15cm squares.

6 Divide the spiced mixture equally between the pastry squares, spreading it diagonally across half the surface of the pastry.

7 Dampen the edges of the pastry with a little water and fold the pastry over to form a triangle shape. Press the pastry edges together firmly to seal the parcels.

8 Place the parcels on a lightly greased baking tray and bake for about 30 minutes until they are golden brown and heated through.

Carrot and Mushroom Roulade

(F V 4)
CALORIES: 353

A delicious and attractive main course which will impress anyone – especially when you tell them it doesn't contain egg yolks. Like most of my recipes, this was developed for Richard who loves soufflé-type dishes but can't eat traditional ones because of the egg yolks. You can adapt the recipe by using a different vegetable, such as spinach, and low-fat soft cheese for the filling.

PREPARATION TIME: 45 MINUTES
COOKING TIME: 30 MINUTES
TEMPERATURE: 200°C/400°F/GAS 6

INGREDIENTS: IMPERIAL/METRIC
2oz/50g polyunsaturated margarine (unhydrogenated)
3oz/75g wholemeal or granary flour
½pt/275ml soya milk (sugar free)
1lb/450g carrots, grated
2tbsp tahini
2tsp marjoram
low-sodium salt
black pepper
2 egg whites
6fl oz/175ml silken tofu, liquidized
8oz/225g mushrooms, wiped and chopped
nutmeg, freshly grated
3oz/75g sunflower seeds, roasted
2oz/50g wholemeal breadcrumbs

METHOD
1 Oil and line an 11in/28cm Swiss roll tin.
2 Melt the margarine in a pan and add 2oz/50g of the flour. Cook for 1 minute, stirring.
3 Remove pan from heat and add the milk gradually, stirring all the time. Bring to the boil and then simmer for about 5 minutes until the sauce thickens.
4 Remove from the heat and add the carrots, tahini, marjoram and pepper.
5 Whisk the egg whites until stiff and carefully fold into the mixture. Spoon into the prepared tin, level, and bake for about 20 minutes until well risen and golden brown.

6 Meanwhile, place the tofu in a saucepan and bring gently to the boil, add the remaining flour and stir. Simmer until the sauce thickens.

7 Add the mushrooms and simmer very gently for 5 minutes. Remove from the heat and add the nutmeg, sunflower seeds, salt and pepper. Leave to cool.

8 When the roulade is cooked turn it out on to a sheet of greaseproof paper sprinkled with the bread-crumbs. Remove the greaseproof lining paper that's come from the tin.

9 Make a shallow cut about ½in/1cm from one of the short ends of the roulade. This will make the rolling up easier.

10 Spoon the mushroom mixture on to the roulade but do not cover the little cut. Then carefully roll the roulade up like a Swiss roll.

11 Gently ease the roulade back towards the centre of the greaseproof paper, then, holding the edges of the greaseproof paper, lift the roulade back on to the Swiss roll tin and return to the oven for 10 minutes to heat through. Slice and serve hot.

Stuffed Aubergines

(F V 4)
CALORIES: 514

Aubergines lend themselves to almost any kind of tasty stuffing.

PREPARATION TIME: 80 MINUTES
COOKING TIME: 40 MINUTES
TEMPERATURE: 200°C/400°F/GAS 6

INGREDIENTS: IMPERIAL/METRIC
2 large aubergines
low-sodium salt
1oz/25g polyunsaturated margarine (unhydrogenated)
1 large onion, peeled and chopped
4oz/125g raisins
5oz/150g wholemeal breadcrumbs
6oz/175g mushrooms, wiped and sliced
2oz/50g sunflower seeds, roasted, roughly chopped
2tbsp fresh parsley, chopped finely
1tsp dried marjoram
1tsp ground coriander
1tbsp tahini
2fl oz/50ml vegetable stock
1tbsp orange zest
1tbsp pumpkin seeds
black pepper

METHOD

1 Wash the aubergines and cut in half lengthways. Carefully scoop out the flesh from each aubergine. Leave about ¼in/6mm thickness to form the 'shell'.

2 Dice the flesh and place in a colander. Sprinkle with salt and shake to make sure that all the pieces have salt on them. Sprinkle the aubergine shells with salt also. Leave for 1 hour.

3 Wash under running water and drain. This process rids the aubergines of their bitter juices.

4 Melt the margarine and add the onion. Fry for 5 minutes until soft but not brown.

5 Add the chopped aubergine and cook for a further 10 minutes.

6 Transfer to a bowl and add all the remaining ingredients. Mix well.

7   Pile the mixture into the aubergine shells and place
    in an ovenproof dish. Bake until the mixture is
    beginning to crisp up and go a golden brown, about
    25 minutes. Serve hot with a crisp salad.

Chick Pea Moussaka

(F V 8)
CALORIES: 281

This recipe comes with the recommendation of a great
friend – a confirmed meat eater!

PREPARATION TIME: 45 MINUTES
COOKING TIME: 50 MINUTES
TEMPERATURE: 190°C/375°F/GAS 5

INGREDIENTS: IMPERIAL/METRIC
2tbsp seasame oil, cold pressed
2 aubergines, sliced ¼in/6mm thick
1oz/25g polyunsaturated margarine (unhydrogenated)
1 onion, peeled and chopped
3 garlic cloves, peeled and crushed
6oz/175g mushrooms, wiped and sliced
2tbsp wholemeal flour
½pt/250ml soya milk (sugar free)
¼pt/150ml vegetable stock
14oz/400g chick peas, cooked
1 lemon, zest of
black pepper

TOPPING
½pt/250ml plain, unsweetened yogurt
2 egg whites
2oz/50g low-fat vegetarian cheese, grated
2oz/50g low-fat soft cheese

METHOD

1 Brush two baking sheets with a little oil. Arrange the aubergine slices in single layers on the baking sheet and brush with the remaining oil. Bake in the pre-heated oven for about 20 minutes until the aubergines are soft.

2 Meanwhile melt the margarine in a saucepan and add the onion. Fry gently for about 5 minutes.

3 Add the garlic and cook for 1 minute.

4 Add the mushrooms and fry for a further 2 minutes.

5 Stir in the flour and cook for 1 minute.

6 Add the soya milk and stock gradually, stirring all the time. Bring to the boil and simmer for 3 minutes.

7 Stir in the chick peas, lemon zest and pepper. Place half this mixture in an ovenproof dish and cover with half the aubergines. Repeat these layers.

8 Beat the yogurt with the egg whites and half the grated cheese. Add the soft cheese in small bits. Pour the cheese mixture on to the aubergines and sprinkle on the remaining grated cheese.

9 Place in the oven and cook until the topping is golden brown, about 15 minutes.

10 Serve hot with a large mixed salad.

TIP BOX

Don't cook pulses and legumes in the water they were soaked in. It could give you flatulence!

Casserole with Dumplings

(F V 4)

PREPARATION TIME: 25 MINUTES
COOKING TIME: I HOUR 10 MINUTES
TEMPERATURE: 200°C/400°F/GAS 6

INGREDIENTS: IMPERIAL/METRIC

Traditional Recipe
CALORIES: 706

1½lb/675g lamb
2tbsp seasoned flour
1tbsp butter
2 onions, peeled and chopped
1lb/450g carrots, peeled and chopped
4oz/125g peas
½pt/300ml water
1 beef stock cube

DUMPLINGS
2oz/50g suet
4oz/125g self-raising flour
1tbsp mixed herbs
black pepper
cold water

Swap Shop Recipe
CALORIES: 525

1tbsp olive oil
2 onions, peeled and chopped
1lb/450g carrots, peeled and chopped
½pt/300ml vegetable stock
4oz/125g peas
1lb/450g chick peas and kidney beans, cooked or tinned

DUMPLINGS
2oz/50g polyunsaturated margarine (unhydrogenated)
4oz/125g plain wholemeal flour
1tsp low-sodium baking powder
1tbsp mixed herbs
black pepper
cold water

METHOD

1 Heat the oil in a large saucepan and gently fry the onion until it is fairly soft. Add the carrots and stir for 1 minute.
2 Add the stock, peas and chick peas, cover and simmer for 30 minutes until the carrots are cooked.
3 Make the dumplings by rubbing the margarine into the flour, baking powder, herbs and seasoning.
4 Add enough cold water to make a firm dough and divide the mixture into eight pieces. Form into balls.
5 Place the casserole mixture in an ovenproof dish and put the dumplings on the top. Cook in the oven for about 40 minutes until the dumplings are golden brown.

Courgettes with Caraway Dumplings

(F V 4)
CALORIES: 647

Richard loves dumplings but cannot eat the traditional ones because of the suet in them, so I invented this recipe for him. The caraway seeds give the dumplings a very distinctive flavour, although fennel seeds could also be used.

PREPARATION TIME: 45 MINUTES
COOKING TIME: 40 MINUTES
TEMPERATURE: 180°C/350°F/GAS 4

INGREDIENTS: IMPERIAL/METRIC
8oz/225g courgettes, washed
3oz/75g polyunsaturated margarine (unhydrogenated)
8oz/225g baby onions, peeled – or large ones, sliced
1lb/450g carrots, washed and sliced
2tbsp paprika
2tbsp potato flour
1pt/500ml vegetable stock
2tsp dried rosemary
black pepper

DUMPLINGS
4oz/100g polyunsaturated margarine (unhydrogenated)
8oz/225g wholemeal flour
4tsp low-sodium baking powder
2tsp caraway seeds
¼pt/150ml silken tofu, liquidized
1tbsp lemon, juice and zest
5tbsp water

METHOD
1 Slice the courgettes and sprinkle with salt. Leave in a
   colander for 30 minutes. Rinse under cold running
   water. Drain.
2 Melt the margarine and fry the courgettes, onions
   and carrots until lightly browned.
3 Add paprika and flour. Fry for 2 minutes, stirring.
4 Gradually stir in the stock, rosemary and pepper.
   Bring to the boil and simmer for 5 minutes.

5   Place in an ovenproof dish.
6   Rub the margarine into the flour and baking powder.
    Add remaining ingredients, except the water.
7   Add the water and form into a firm ball. Divide into
    16 small round dumplings and place on top of the
    courgette mixture.
8   Sprinkle the dumplings with a few extra caraway
    seeds.
9   Cook in the oven for about 40 minutes until the
    dumplings are well risen and golden brown.

TIP BOX

Try using herbs, spices and fruit zest as seasoning
instead of salt, it's healthier and helps ring the
changes.

Festive Loaf

(F V 4)
CALORIES: 512

I invented this recipe mid-morning one Christmas Day
and, yes, it was for our Christmas dinner. Thank goodness it worked! I wanted to capture the taste of traditional Christmas fare and so the sage and cranberries are
of paramount importance to this dish – hence the name.

PREPARATION TIME: 90 MINUTES
COOKING TIME: 90 MINUTES
TEMPERATURE: 180°C/350°F/GAS 4

INGREDIENTS: IMPERIAL/METRIC

Mushroom and sage layer
2tbsp extra virgin olive oil
1 onion, peeled and chopped
6oz/175g mushrooms, wiped and sliced
2oz/50g wholemeal breadcrumbs
2tsp dried sage
1tbsp sunflower seeds, roasted
1tbsp tahini
1tbsp soya milk
black pepper and low-sodium salt

Cranberry and apricot layer
1tbsp extra virgin olive oil
1 onion, peeled and chopped
4oz/100g cranberries, washed
2oz/50g wholemeal breadcrumbs
2oz/50g sunflower seeds, roasted and ground
2oz/50g dried apricots, soaked and
chopped (unsulphurated)
1tbsp tahini
1tbsp soya milk
black pepper and low-sodium salt

Split pea layer
1tbsp extra virgin olive oil
1 onion, peeled and chopped
6oz/175g yellow split peas, washed, soaked and cooked
1 egg white
black pepper and low-sodium salt

METHOD
1 Grease and line a 2lb/900g loaf tin.
2 *Mushroom and sage layer*. Heat the oil and fry the

onion until soft but not browned, about 5 minutes. Add the mushrooms and fry for 3 minutes.

3 In a bowl mix all the remaining ingredients and put to one side.

4 *Cranberry and apricot layer*. Heat the oil and fry the onion until soft.

5 In a bowl mix in all the remaining ingredients and put to one side.

6 *Split pea layer*. Heat the oil and fry the onion until soft and add to the split peas.

7 Beat the egg white and add to the mixture. Season to taste.

8 Place the mushroom mixture in the base of the tin, pressing it down firmly with the back of a spoon.

9 Then add the cranberry layer, pressing down very firmly.

10 Add the split pea layer and press down firmly. Cover with greased foil and bake for 1 hour 30 minutes. Allow to cool for at least 10 minutes before turning out of the tin. This is lovely served, hot or cold, with a cranberry sauce.

Mushroom Stroganoff

(v 4)
CALORIES: 152

Many years ago when I ate meat a good stroganoff was my favourite meal. Not to lose out I invented this dish which contains none of the 'baddies' and tastes delicious.

PREPARATION TIME: 15 MINUTES
COOKING TIME: 30 MINUTES

INGREDIENTS: IMPERIAL/METRIC
2oz/50g polyunsaturated margarine (unhydrogenated)
1 large onion, peeled and sliced
2 garlic cloves, peeled and crushed
1lb/450g button mushrooms, wiped and sliced
6oz/175g fresh tomatoes, wiped and sliced
¼pt/150ml silken tofu, liquidized
1tbsp fresh chives, chopped
black pepper and low-sodium salt

METHOD

1 Heat the margarine and add the onion and garlic. Fry gently for 5 minutes.
2 Add the mushrooms and cook for 3 minutes.
3 Add the tomatoes and cook gently for 5 minutes.
4 Stir in the tofu and chives and gently heat through, but do not allow to boil.
5 Season to taste and serve hot with brown rice.

TIP BOX

Bruise or crush the garlic clove to obtain the strongest flavour.

Stuffed Savoy

(F V 4)
CALORIES: 150

Impressive parcels filled with layers of different flavours and textures.

PREPARATION TIME: 35 MINUTES
COOKING TIME: 60 MINUTES
TEMPERATURE: 180°C/350°F/GAS 4

INGREDIENTS: IMPERIAL/METRIC
4 outer leaves from a Savoy cabbage, washed
1 large carrot, washed
2tbsp extra virgin olive oil
1tbsp onion, peeled and finely sliced
3tbsp wholemeal breadcrumbs
2tbsp sunflower seeds, roasted
1tsp tamari (strong soy sauce)
½ lemon, zest and juice
3tbsp silken tofu, liquidized
1tbsp wholemeal flour
4oz/125g mushrooms, wiped and finely chopped
1tsp nutmeg, freshly grated
black pepper and low-sodium salt

METHOD
1 Plunge the cabbage leaves into boiling water for 5 minutes then place under cold running water to fix colour. Carefully cut out the central stalks.
2 Cut the carrot into matchstick lengths, about ¼in/6mm thick. Cook in boiling water for about 10 minutes. Drain and reserve liquid for stock.
3 Heat the oil, add the onion, and fry gently for 5 minutes.

4 Mix together the onion, breadcrumbs, seeds, tamari, lemon zest and juice.

5 Place the tofu in a small saucepan. Heat through and add the flour, stirring, until the sauce thickens. Add the mushrooms and cook for 3 minutes.

6 Remove from heat and add the nutmeg and seasoning. Leave to cool.

7 Spread the cabbage leaves out flat. Divide the breadcrumb mixture between them, placing the mixture in the centre of each leaf. Press down very firmly.

8 Arrange a layer of carrot on the top.

9 Finish with a layer of tofu. Carefully fold up the cabbage leaf tightly, like a parcel.

10 Bake in a shallow ovenproof dish, with a little hot water in the base, for 30 minutes. Serve with fresh vegetables and some garlic and tofu dip (page 66) to which you have added a good squeeze of lemon juice.

TIP BOX

Increase your fibre intake gradually over some weeks rather than suddenly. This way you will avoid initial digestive problems.

Tomato and Carrot Flan

(F V)
CALORIES: 131

A very colourful flan with lots of taste and a variety of textures.

PREPARATION TIME: 40 MINUTES
COOKING TIME: 30 MINUTES
TEMPERATURE: 200°C/400°F/GAS 6
SETTING TIME: 60 minutes

INGREDIENTS: IMPERIAL/METRIC
1 recipe low-fat pastry (see page 156)
1tbsp extra virgin olive oil
3oz/75g onion, peeled and chopped
2 garlic cloves, peeled and crushed
8oz/225g tomatoes, washed and chopped
4oz/125g carrots, washed and grated
4oz/125g red lentils, washed and cooked
1tbsp tomato purée
½pt/250ml water
black pepper
1tbsp fresh mint, washed and chopped
1tbsp Gelozone

METHOD

1   Roll out the pastry and line an 8in/20cm flan dish. Prick the base.

2   Bake in the hottest part of the oven for 20 minutes. (Even in fan-assisted ovens the top is usually the hottest part. It is important for the sides of the flan to cook, otherwise they will collapse.) Leave to cool.

3   Heat the oil in a medium-sized saucepan. Fry the onion and garlic for 5 minutes.

4   Add the tomatoes, carrots, lentils, tomato purée and water. Season with black pepper. Bring to the boil and gently simmer.

5   Add the mint and stir in the Gelozone very quickly with a fork to ensure it dissolves completely. Simmer for 3 minutes.

6   Pour the mixture into the pastry case and leave for about 1 hour to set.

Vegetable Lasagne

(F V 8)
CALORIES: 152

Many people love a lasagne. This one is very colourful with the reds and greens of the peppers against the creamy white sauce.

PREPARATION TIME: 45 MINUTES
COOKING TIME: 40 MINUTES
TEMPERATURE: 190°C/375°F/GAS 5

INGREDIENTS: IMPERIAL/METRIC
8oz/225g carrots, washed and diced
8oz/225g courgettes, washed and sliced
1 onion, peeled and chopped
3 garlic cloves, peeled and crushed
1 red pepper, washed, seeded and sliced
1 green pepper, washed, seeded and sliced
¼pt/150ml vegetable stock
1oz/25g polyunsaturated margarine (unhydrogenated)
2tbsp wholemeal flour
½pt/250ml soya milk (sugar free)
black pepper and low-sodium salt
2tsp dried thyme
2tsp dried chives
6oz/175g wholewheat lasagne
3oz/75g low-fat vegetarian cheese, grated
3oz/75g low-fat vegetarian soft cheese

METHOD

1 Place the first six ingredients in a saucepan with the stock. Bring to the boil and simmer for 10 minutes, covered.

2 Melt the margarine in a pan and add the flour. Cook for 1 minute, stirring all the time. Remove from the heat.

3 Gradually stir in the milk. Return to the heat, bring to the boil and simmer for about 5 minutes, until the sauce thickens, stirring frequently. Season and add the herbs.

4 Cook the lasagne as directed on the packet. Drain.

5 In a large, shallow, ovenproof dish make alternate layers of vegetables, lasagne and cheese – finishing with a layer of lasagne.

6 Pour on the sauce and bake until piping hot and bubbling – about 40 minutes.

7 Serve with a crisp mixed salad.

Spiced Vegetable Bake

(F V 4)
CALORIES: 251

This dish, a subtle blend of spices and vegetables with a slightly tart topping, was invented on a wing and a prayer – literally! Unexpected guests, requiring an evening meal, arrived and I had to conjure up something for them fast. It's now a regular on the menu at Harrow Ings.

PREPARATION TIME: 40 MINUTES
COOKING TIME: 55 MINUTES
TEMPERATURE: 200°C/400°F/GAS 6

INGREDIENTS: IMPERIAL/METRIC
1 aubergine
3tbsp extra virgin olive oil (2tbsp for frying,
1tbsp for the aubergines)
2tsp cumin seeds
2tsp garam masala
2 onions, peeled and sliced
3 garlic cloves, peeled and crushed
12oz/350g pumpkin, peeled, seeded and diced *or* swede,
peeled and diced
2tbsp raisins
3tbsp fresh parsley, chopped
black pepper
8oz/225g fromage frais (1% fat variety)

METHOD
1 Wipe and slice the aubergine into rounds of about
¼in/6mm thickness. Brush a baking tray with oil
and place the aubergine slices on to it. Brush with
oil. Cook in the oven for about 30 minutes. Leave to
one side.
2 Heat the remaining oil in a large saucepan. Add the
cumin seeds and garam masala and cook for 3
minutes.
3 Add the onion and garlic and fry gently for 5
minutes.
4 Add the pumpkin (or swede). Stir well and cook,
covered, for about 30 minutes – until the pumpkin is
just tender.
5 Add the raisins and cook gently for 10 minutes.
6 Remove from the heat and stir in the chopped parsley and seasoning.
7 Divide the pumpkin mixture between four indivi-

dual ovenproof dishes. Place a layer of aubergine on
the top of each.

8 Spoon the fromage frais over the mixture.

9 Place in the oven and cook for just a few minutes
until the topping is golden brown and just beginning
to crisp up.

10 Serve hot together with a baked potato and parsnips
sprinkled with lemon juice.

TIP BOX

Garlic has been known for its healing powers for
centuries in many cultures. Garlic reduces the
LDL type of cholesterol, the 'bad' one, and
increases the 'good' type, HDL, and is also
beneficial in treating heart disease. It is also well
known for its antibiotic qualities.

Vegetable Crumble

(F V 4)
CALORIES: 310

The crunchy topping has a nutty taste and the garlic
gives it a nice 'bite'. The vegetables taste better if they
are slightly undercooked.

PREPARATION TIME: 25 MINUTES
COOKING TIME: 30 MINUTES
TEMPERATURE: 180°C/350°F/GAS 4

INGREDIENTS: IMPERIAL/METRIC
2oz/50g polyunsaturated margarine (unhydrogenated)
1 large onion, peeled and chopped
1 red pepper, washed, seeded and diced
1 green pepper, washed, seeded and diced
6oz/175g button mushrooms, wiped and diced
black pepper and low-sodium salt
6oz/175g fresh tomatoes, washed and diced

TOPPING
6oz/175g wholemeal breadcrumbs
2 garlic cloves, peeled and crushed
4oz/125g mixed seeds (pumpkin, sunflower, for
example), ground

METHOD
1   Melt the margarine in a saucepan and fry the onion
    and peppers for 3 minutes, gently.
2   Add the mushrooms and seasoning. Cook for 3
    minutes.
3   Add the tomatoes and cook for 5 minutes, stirring
    gently.
4   Place the mixture in four individual ovenproof
    dishes.
5   Mix together all the topping ingredients and divide it
    between the four dishes.
6   Bake until heated through and golden brown on the
    top, about 20 minutes.
7   Serve with jacket potatoes and a selection of lightly
    steamed vegetables.

TIP BOX

In spite of its name, buckwheat flour does not
contain wheat and can be used by coeliacs.

Basic Buckwheat Pancake Mixture

(F V 4)
CALORIES: 182

Pancakes are wonderful because they are versatile, as well as quick and easy to make. Try using different fillings and sauces – the combinations are endless. Buckwheat flour gives the pancakes a 'nutty' flavour which I find delicious, but you can use other flours and each will give a subtly different taste.

PREPARATION TIME: 10 MINUTES
COOKING TIME: 10 MINUTES

INGREDIENTS: IMPERIAL/METRIC
4oz/125g buckwheat flour
½pt/250ml soya milk (sugar free)
black pepper
2tsp extra virgin olive oil
little oil for frying

METHOD

1 Sift the flour into a bowl.
2 Gradually add the milk and beat well until the mixture is smooth.
3 Add the black pepper and oil.
4 Continue to whisk the mixture to let more air into the batter.
5 Melt a little oil in a non-stick frying pan and pour in a thin layer of the batter. Cook gently on one side, and when cooked toss, or turn with a wooden spatula, and cook the other side.
6 Keep the pancakes warm while you make the remainder. A good way to do this is to turn the grill

on high before you start making the pancakes. Then, just before the first one is cooked, turn the grill low and slip the pancakes on to a plate under the grill as you make them.

Broccoli and Mushroom Pancake Filling

(F V 4)
CALORIES: 118

Just one of many possible pancake fillings to give you inspiration!

PREPARATION TIME: 15 MINUTES
COOKING TIME: 25 MINUTES
TEMPERATURE: 150°C/300°F/GAS 2

INGREDIENTS: IMPERIAL/METRIC
4oz/125g broccoli, washed and cut into small florets
8oz/225g mushrooms, wiped and sliced
3oz/75g sunflower seeds, roasted
8oz/225g fromage frais (1% fat variety)
2oz/50g low-fat vegetarian cheese, grated
black pepper

METHOD
1   Steam the broccoli for about 5 minutes.
2   Make the pancakes as in the recipe on page 180.
3   Mix together the mushrooms, broccoli, seeds, cheeses and black pepper.
4   Place a spoonful of the mixture on half of each pancake.
5   Fold the pancake to cover the mixture.

6   Place the pancakes in a shallow ovenproof dish and
     bake for about 20 minutes until heated through.

Butter Bean Rissoles

(F V 4)
CALORIES: 229

A delicate mixture of pale greens and pale yellows, these
rissoles are crisp on the outside and beautifully soft on
the inside.

PREPARATION TIME: 20 MINUTES
COOKING TIME: 8 MINUTES

INGREDIENTS: IMPERIAL/METRIC
8oz/225g butter beans, soaked and cooked – reserve the
liquid
1tbsp tahini
3tbsp fresh parsley, chopped
3 garlic cloves, peeled and crushed
1tsp dried basil
1tsp saffron
1tbsp soya milk (sugar free)
1tbsp sesame seeds or millet flakes
1tbsp extra virgin olive oil

METHOD
1   Mash the butter beans with 4 tbsp of the reserved
     cooking liquid.
2   Add the tahini, parsley, garlic, basil and saffron.
     Mix well.
3   Form into eight rissole (burger) shapes.

4   Brush with the soya milk and coat with the seeds or
     flakes.
5   Shallow fry in the oil for 4 minutes on each side.
6   Serve hot with either a salad or vegetables.

Tomato and Seed Rissoles

(F V 4)
CALORIES: 272

These rissoles are also good sandwiched inside a wholemeal bap with some onions and relish.

PREPARATION TIME: 15 MINUTES
COOKING TIME: 10 MINUTES

INGREDIENTS: IMPERIAL/METRIC
4oz/125g sunflower seeds, ground
2oz/50g vegetarian low-fat cheese, grated
2oz/50g vegetarian low-fat soft cheese
4 tomatoes, chopped
2 garlic cloves, peeled and crushed
1tbsp tomato purée (sugar free)
1oz/25g onion, grated
2tsp mixed herbs
1tbsp tahini
3oz/75g wholemeal breadcrumbs
1tbsp soya milk (sugar free)
2tbsp olive oil for frying
1 lemon, zest and juice
black pepper

METHOD

1 Mix all the ingredients, except for the soya milk and 1oz/25g of the breadcrumbs, together in a bowl.
2 Form into eight evenly sized rissole (burger) shapes.
3 Brush each with a little soya milk and coat with the remaining breadcrumbs.
4 Shallow fry until they are crisp and golden brown.
5 Serve hot, garnished with slices of tomato.

CHAPTER NINE

NAKED VEGETABLES

ALL TOO often the vegetables accompanying a main meal are not given a second thought. Rather than being there just to fill up the plate they should complement the main dish and supply various nutrients.

Fresh vegetables in season are wonderful and take very little preparation and cooking. Most fresh vegetables can be cooked as quickly as tinned vegetables. The advantage of using fresh is that you retain important vitamins, minerals and fibre, without the problem of added sugar, salt and preservatives. The taste is totally different as well. Fresh vegetables are tasty, crisp and appetizing, and tend to be cheaper than their tinned counterparts.

There are many interesting vegetables on the market these days from all over the world and they are certainly worth trying. Experiment with them – be adventurous for it is well worth the effort.

COMMON PROBLEMS

The most common problem is overcooking. The only thing worse than looking at a plate of limp, lifeless vegetables is eating them. Vegetables should be fresh looking, crisp and colourful. The secret is to cook them for the shortest time possible. This retains not only their flavour but also their nutrients.

The best way to cook vegetables is by steaming them briefly over a pan of boiling water. They should be steamed until just tender but retaining their crispness. Keep testing vegetables by piercing them with a sharp pointed knife. Vegetables which are boiled lose a lot of their nutrients in the cooking liquid and become limp.

When preparing vegetables cut away as little as possible. Most vegetables need only washing or at the most scraping. Cut vegetables like carrots or courgettes lengthways rather than in circles. They not only cook more quickly but they also retain more of their nutrients.

From the way vegetables so often get plonked on a plate, you'd think their presentation was a problem, but it really isn't. When you are planning a meal think of the colours that will be together on the plate. Will they complement each other? Will the plate look too dull? I like to see contrasting colours such as the dark green of spring cabbage with the vibrant orange of carrots. I would never serve cauliflower, sweetcorn and mashed potato on the same plate – the colours are much too similar.

Once you have thought about the colours then you have to arrange them attractively on the plate, bearing in mind not only colour but also textures and shapes. Serve chopped root vegetables with leafy vegetables. And if one of the vegetables is served with a sauce the others should be served *au naturel*. It is easy to overdo the use of sauces. There is nothing wrong with 'naked' vegetables – they taste delicious.

Aubergine with Tomatoes

(F V 8)
CALORIES: 71

Aubergine and tomatoes provide a colourful accompaniment to any main course. In fact, served with garlic bread, this dish is substantial enough for a main course.

PREPARATION TIME: 20 MINUTES
COOKING TIME: 25 MINUTES
TEMPERATURE: 230°C/460°F/GAS 8

INGREDIENTS: IMPERIAL/METRIC
2 aubergines, washed
1 tbsp sesame seed oil
8oz/225g tomatoes, washed and halved
2tsp dried basil
black pepper and low-sodium salt

METHOD
1 Slice the aubergines into rings ¼in/6mm thick.
2 Brush three baking trays with the oil.
3 Arrange the aubergine slices on two of the baking trays, making sure that you do not overlap them. Brush lightly with oil.
4 Arrange the tomato halves on the remaining baking tray and sprinkle with the basil.
5 Bake for 15 minutes.
6 Mix the aubergines and tomatoes together with the seasonings and arrange in a warm serving dish.

Broccoli with Mint and Yogurt

(v 4)
CALORIES: 42

Yogurt and fresh mint go very well together and make an interesting dressing for salads and vegetables alike.

PREPARATION TIME: 20 MINUTES
COOKING TIME: 15 MINUTES

INGREDIENTS: IMPERIAL/METRIC
1lb/450g broccoli, well washed
¼pt/150ml natural, unsweetened low-fat yogurt
1tbsp fresh mint, chopped
black pepper
1 sprig fresh mint

METHOD

1 Place the broccoli in a steamer and steam over a pan of boiling water for 15 minutes.
2 Gently heat the yogurt in a small saucepan. Add the mint and pepper.
3 Place the broccoli in a warm serving dish and pour over the mint and yogurt sauce.
4 Garnish with a sprig of mint.

TIP BOX

Vegetables should be used as quickly as possible after being picked, otherwise they lose nutrients.

Carrots with Orange and Ginger

(F V 4)

CALORIES: 44

The carrots absorb the orange juice and ginger during cooking which gives them a distinctive flavour. By serving with the cooking juice, you will retain the nutrients lost during cooking.

PREPARATION TIME: 10 MINUTES

COOKING TIME: 20 MINUTES

INGREDIENTS: IMPERIAL/METRIC

1lb/450g carrots, washed

2tsp ground ginger

black pepper

½pt/250ml orange juice, unsweetened

1tsp stem ginger, chopped

METHOD

1 Cut the carrots into fingers about 2in/5cm long and ¼in/6mm thick.
2 Place half the carrots in a medium-sized saucepan. Sprinkle with black pepper and half the ground ginger.
3 Top with the remaining carrots and sprinkle on the remaining ground ginger and the black pepper.
4 Pour on the orange juice.
5 Bring to the boil and simmer for about 20 minutes, until the carrots are tender but not soft.
6 Place the carrots and the juice in a scrving dish and sprinkle the chopped stem ginger on the top.

Cheese and Celery Baked Potato

(V 4)
CALORIES: 81

Baked potatoes lend themselves to a variety of fillings.
This one combines the flavours of cheese and celery.

PREPARATION TIME: 20 MINUTES
COOKING TIME: 70 MINUTES
TEMPERATURE: 200°C/400°F/GAS 6

INGREDIENTS: IMPERIAL/METRIC
4 potatoes, large enough to bake, washed
2 celery sticks, washed and grated
4oz/125g vegetarian low-fat soft cheese
2tsp paprika pepper
1tbsp fresh chives, chopped

METHOD

1   Place a skewer through each potato and bake in the
    oven for about 1 hour, or until cooked through.
2   Meanwhile mix together the remaining ingredients,
    keeping the chives for garnish.
3   Carefully scoop out the cooked potato leaving a shell.
4   Add this potato to the cheese mixture and mix well.
5   Pile this mixture into each of the potato shells and
    return to the oven for 10 minutes.
6   Sprinkle each with some chopped fresh chives.

Leeks with Lemon and Raisins

(F V 4)
CALORIES: 206

Unusual and tasty, the raisins add a sweetness to the leeks and the lemon adds a nice tang.

PREPARATION TIME: 15 MINUTES
COOKING TIME: 7 MINUTES

INGREDIENTS: IMPERIAL/METRIC
1tbsp sesame seed oil
1lb/450g leeks, washed well and chopped
2tsp caraway seeds
2tbsp raisins
black pepper
2 lemons, juice and zest

METHOD
1 Heat the oil in a wok or large frying pan.
2 Add the leeks and stir-fry for 5 minutes.
3 Add the caraway seeds, raisins and black pepper. Stir-fry for 2 minutes.
4 Remove from the heat and arrange the leeks in a serving dish.
5 Pour over the lemon juice and sprinkle on the zest. Combine well and serve.

Mangetout and Mushrooms

(F V 4)
CALORIES: 64

Also known as snow peas, these are the peas that you eat whole – pod and all – and they cook in no time.

PREPARATION TIME: 5 MINUTES
COOKING TIME: 5 MINUTES

INGREDIENTS: IMPERIAL/METRIC
½tbsp sesame seed oil, cold pressed
8oz/225g button mushrooms, wiped
8oz/225g mangetout peas, washed
black pepper

METHOD
1   Heat the oil in a wok or large frying pan.
2   Add the mushrooms and stir-fry for 2 minutes.
3   Add the mangetout and stir-fry for 1 minute.
4   Add the black pepper and stir-fry for 1 minute.
5   Arrange in a warm shallow dish and serve.

Okra and Mushrooms

(F V 4)
CALORIES: 44

Okra is sometimes called 'ladies' fingers' which aptly
describes its shape. When sliced it becomes sticky, so is
really nicer whole.

PREPARATION TIME: 10 MINUTES
COOKING TIME: 5 MINUTES

INGREDIENTS: IMPERIAL/METRIC
½tbsp sesame seed oil
1tsp cumin seeds
1tsp garam masala
8oz/225g okra, washed and trimmed
8oz/225g mushrooms, wiped and sliced

METHOD
1 Heat the oil in a wok or large frying pan.
2 Add the cumin seeds and garam masala. Fry for 1
   minute.
3 Add the okra and stir-fry for 2 minutes.
4 Add the mushrooms and stir-fry for 2 minutes.
5 Arrange in a warm dish and serve.

Spinach with Apple

(v 4)

CALORIES: 36

An unusual mixture of distinctive flavours which is quick and easy to prepare.

PREPARATION TIME: 6 MINUTES
COOKING TIME: 5 MINUTES

INGREDIENTS: IMPERIAL/METRIC
12oz/350g spinach, washed and chopped
4oz/125g red apple, washed, cored and thickly sliced

METHOD
1   Place the spinach and apple together in a steamer.
2   Steam over a pan of boiling water for 5 minutes.
3   Serve at once.

CHAPTER TEN

SALAD DAYS

SALADS are so very versatile that you could have a different one every day of the year. The combination of colours, flavours and textures is endless. Salads can be used as main courses, starters or snacks.

And as for ingredients, you can add almost anything you happen to have in your larder to a salad – beans, lentils, vegetables, fruit, seeds. Use herbs, spices and fruit zests (scrub fruits well before you zest them) for subtle flavours. The addition of seeds, sprouted beans, raw fruit and raw vegetables will give the salad a crisp and crunchy texture. If you want a smooth, rich, creamy salad then use fromage frais, low-fat natural yogurt or tofu as the base and just mix in chopped or puréed fruit and vegetables.

I love making salads. You can let your artistic streak show and conjure up a work of art. In fact, one of our guests who opted for a vegetarian breakfast exclaimed, 'I can't eat this.' I thought, oops, what's wrong with it. 'It looks too attractive to eat. Just a minute, I'll go and get my camera.' Yes, he did take a photograph of his breakfast – and did so each morning of his stay with us. After that all the traditional breakfast-eaters wanted the vegetarian breakfast for the remainder of their stay!

COMMON PROBLEMS

Too many people think a salad is a piece of lettuce, a slice of tomato, a little cucumber and an onion ring or two, put in a limp pile on your plate. No wonder salad has a bad reputation! Break away from the lettuce and cucumber brigade and experiment with unusual combinations of foods. If you're feeling hesitant, try some of the following recipes, and you'll soon go on to make your own inventions. Presentation really comes to the fore when making salads. You can present a salad beautifully arranged on a single lettuce leaf or nestling in several chicory leaves. Curled spring onions give added height and an extra dimension. Well-placed 'radish flowers', 'curly celery boats' and 'carrot roses' add a real touch of class – they never fail to impress. And you definitely don't have to spend ages getting the salads ready. I present salads like these as part of my vegetarian breakfasts and they are all made before the meal – if they required hours of work on presentation I couldn't do it!

Stuffed Apples

(v 4)

CALORIES: 140

A lovely refreshing salad which combines soft cheese, fruits and seeds.

PREPARATION TIME: 15 MINUTES

INGREDIENTS: IMPERIAL/METRIC
8oz/225g low-fat soft cheese
4oz/125g fresh pineapple, peeled and cubed
1oz/25g sunflower seeds
3oz/75g fresh apricots, washed, stoned and chopped
2 large dessert apples, washed and cored
2tsp lemon juice
8oz/225g carrot, washed and grated

METHOD
1   Combine the low-fat soft cheese with the pineapple, sunflower seeds and apricots.
2   Cut the apples in half down from the stalk, and carefully scoop out the apple to form four shells. Coat all the apple with the lemon juice.
3   Dice the apple flesh, mix with the soft cheese mixture and pile into the apple shells.
4   Place the grated carrot on a large plate and arrange the stuffed apples on the top. Serve well chilled.

Courgette and Melon Salad

(v 4)
CALORIES: 82

The tofu gives the salad a nice, light creamy texture without overpowering the taste of the fruits and vegetables.

PREPARATION TIME: 10 MINUTES

INGREDIENTS: IMPERIAL/METRIC
8fl oz/225ml silken tofu, liquidized
8oz/225g courgettes, washed and grated
8oz/225g melon, peeled and chopped
1oz/25g dried prunes, washed, stoned and chopped
1oz/25g dried dates, washed, pitted and chopped
1tsp honey (optional)
4oz/125g chicory, washed

METHOD
1   Mix all the ingredients, except the chicory, together.
2   Pile the mixture on to a serving dish and arrange the chicory in it. The consistency of mixture will enable you to stand the chicory upright – just stick it in. Arrange some chicory around the edge of the dish.

Creamy Vegetable Salad

(4)
CALORIES: 115

Fromage frais tastes so rich and creamy that it's hard to believe it contains less than 1 per cent fat.

PREPARATION TIME: 15 MINUTES

INGREDIENTS: IMPERIAL/METRIC
8oz/225g fromage frais (1% fat variety)
4oz/125g celery, washed and chopped
2oz/50g chick peas, soaked and cooked
2oz/50g red lentils, washed and cooked
2oz/50g parsnips, peeled and grated
4oz/125g red peppers, washed, seeded and chopped
parsley sprigs or watercress to garnish

METHOD

Mix all the ingredients together, put in a bowl or on a serving dish and garnish with some fresh parsley or watercress.

Crunchy Salad

(V 4)
CALORIES: 71

If you like crunchy salads you will enjoy this one – it is wonderfully refreshing.

PREPARATION TIME: 15 MINUTES

INGREDIENTS: IMPERIAL/METRIC
8oz/225g courgettes, washed and grated
1 red apple, washed, cored and sliced
2 celery sticks, washed and chopped
1 green pepper, washed, seeded and chopped
2tbsp pumpkin seeds
2tbsp sunflower seeds
1 lemon, zest and juice

METHOD

Mix all the ingredients together well and serve in a large shallow dish.

TIP BOX

Cut the top off a tomato and carefully hollow out the middle. Stuff with a mixture of low-fat soft cheese and herbs or with pulses and sprouted beans. Replace their 'caps' and serve with a salad.

Mangetout and Okra Salad

(v 4)
CALORIES: 65

A beautifully crisp and colourful salad which has a nice freshness about it.

PREPARATION TIME: 15 MINUTES
COOKING TIME: 5 MINUTES

INGREDIENTS: IMPERIAL/METRIC
4oz/100g okra, washed and trimmed
4oz/100g carrot, washed
4oz/100g mangetout, washed and trimmed
2oz/50g sunflower seeds
2oz/50g spring onions, washed and curled

METHOD

1   Steam the okra for 5 minutes. Run under cold water to fix the colour.

2 Cut the carrots into long, thin sticks with a sharp knife.
3 Mix the first four ingredients together and pile into a serving dish. Stand the 'curled' onions like weeping willows around the salad base. To curl the spring onions, wash them and trim off the roots and any discoloured or lanky outer leaves, so you have a nice straight green and white length. Then split the onion lengthways, almost to the base, with two downward, slightly angled cuts, so the green part will curl downwards. Plunge into iced water for 15 minutes.

Chicory and Apple Salad

(v 6)

PREPARATION TIME: 15 MINUTES

INGREDIENTS: IMPERIAL/METRIC

Traditional Recipe
CALORIES: 281

1 large green apple, peeled and chopped
1 large red apple, peeled and chopped
1 lemon, juiced
8oz/225g chicory, sliced
4oz/125g black grapes, seeded
4oz/125g ham, cubed

DRESSING
3oz/75g Danish blue cheese
¼pt/150ml double cream
2tsp fresh dill, chopped

Swap Shop Recipe
CALORIES: 128

1 large green apple, washed and chopped
1 large red apple, washed and chopped
1 lemon, juiced
8oz/225g chicory
4oz/125g black grapes, seeded
4oz/125g chicken, cubed

DRESSING
3oz/75g Roule light cheese
¼pt/150ml low-fat natural yogurt
2tsp fresh dill, chopped

METHOD
1 Place the apples in a bowl with the lemon juice and toss well. Add the chicory, grapes and chicken – mix well.
2 Make the dressing: beat the cheese and gradually add the yogurt – stir well. Add the dill.
3 Pour the dressing over the salad and toss.

Burghul and Tuna Salad

(v 6)
CALORIES: 190

What a wonderful combination – you must try this one!
Burghul wheat is also called bulgar. It is wheat that has
been cracked by boiling and so absorbs moisture easily.

PREPARATION TIME: 15 MINUTES

INGREDIENTS: IMPERIAL/METRIC
4oz/125g burghul wheat, soaked in cold water for 30
minutes and drained well
4oz/125g tuna fish, left in chunks
6 spring onions, chopped
2 tomatoes, chopped
1 orange, peeled and chopped
2tbsp orange juice
1tbsp fresh chives, chopped
1tbsp fresh mint, chopped
black pepper

METHOD
1 Mix together the burghul wheat, tuna, spring
onions, tomatoes and orange chunks.
2 Blend together the orange juice, chives, mint and
pepper.
3 Pour over the wheat mixture and leave for 5 minutes.
Serve.

Walnut Coleslaw

(v 4)

PREPARATION TIME: 10 MINUTES
COOKING TIME: 2 MINUTES

INGREDIENTS: IMPERIAL/METRIC

Traditional Recipe
CALORIES: 347

12oz/350g white cabbage, shredded
2oz/50g cashew nuts, chopped
1 apple, peeled and chopped
3oz/75g black grapes, seeded
2tsp caraway seeds, toasted and crushed

DRESSING
¼pt/150ml double cream
1tbsp mayonnaise
2tsp clear honey
½tsp mustard powder
1tbsp cornflour
1 lemon, juice and zest
salt and pepper

Swap Shop Recipe
CALORIES: 191

12oz/350g white cabbage, shredded
2oz/50g walnuts, chopped
1 apple, washed and chopped
3oz/75g black grapes, seeded
2tsp caraway seeds, toasted and crushed

DRESSING
¼pt/150ml low-fat natural yogurt
1tbsp low-calorie mayonnaise
2tsp clear honey
½tsp mustard powder
1tbsp cornflour
low-sodium salt
black pepper
1 lemon, juice and zest

METHOD

1 Make the dressing by mixing the yogurt, mayonnaise, honey, mustard, cornflour and seasoning to a paste with 1tbsp cold water. Put the mixture into the top of a double saucepan over simmering water. Stir constantly for 2 minutes. Add the lemon juice and zest, stirring well. Leave to cool.

2 Mix together the salad ingredients and stir in the dressing. Toss well and serve.

CHAPTER ELEVEN

FINISHING TOUCHES

TO MOST people a meal without a sweet to end it is not a 'proper meal'. I like nothing better than fresh fruits of the season – either plain or in a fruit salad. But for many people used to traditional food, this is not enough.

My husband has a very sweet tooth and so over the years I have developed recipes for desserts which will satisfy him without being hazardous to health. The traditional types of desserts are extremely unhealthy as they are usually very high in sugar and fats and low in fibre. The recipes in this chapter are all extremely low in fat and sugar and quite high in fibre. You will notice immediately that two of the most popular ingredients used for traditional sweets, cream and sugar, are absent from my recipes. Both are very easy to replace with healthier alternatives, but this does not mean that the desserts will be tart or lack flavour.

Take advantage of fresh seasonal fruits by using them in mousses and crumbles. There are many interesting and exotic fruits with which to experiment. I like to mix fresh fruits with dried fruits as this gives a nice texture to the dish and increases the fibre content. To serve with your dessert try low-fat natural yogurt, tofu or a soya-based topping instead of cream or custard.

SWAP SHOP RECIPES

Converting traditional desserts into healthier versions is relatively easy. The main ingredients to change are sugar and cream.

The substitutes I used for sugar are dried dates, concentrated fruit juices and honey. These act as sweeteners but have fewer calories and more nutrients than sugar.

Instead of cream I use silken tofu, fromage frais, concentrated soya milk or low-fat natural yogurt. The desserts will be just as rich and creamy as traditional ones made with cream but will have the benefit of fewer calories and far less fat.

The swap shop recipes will give you an idea of the substitution process in action.

Fruit Crumble

(F V 4)

**PREPARATION TIME: 20 MINUTES
COOKING TIME: 25 MINUTES
TEMPERATURE: 200°C/400°F/GAS 6**

INGREDIENTS: IMPERIAL/METRIC

Traditional Recipe
CALORIES: 395

2oz/50g butter
6oz/175g plain flour
4oz/125g sugar
1oz/25g peanuts
8oz/225g cooking apples, peeled and sliced
8oz/225g raspberries, washed

Swap Shop Recipe
CALORIES: 271

2oz/50g polyunsaturated margarine (unhydrogenated)
4oz/125g plain wholemeal flour
2oz/50g oats
1oz/25g muscovado sugar
2tsp ground cinnamon
1tsp mixed spice
1oz/25g stoned dates, chopped
½oz/15g walnuts, chopped
8oz/225g eating apples, washed and sliced
8oz/225g raspberries, washed

METHOD

1 Rub the margarine into the flour until it resembles breadcrumbs. Stir in the oats, sugar, cinnamon, mixed spice, dates and walnuts. Mix well.
2 Place the apples and raspberries in a 1½pt/900ml pie dish and cover with the crumble mixture.
3 Bake until golden brown, about 25 minutes.

Dried Fruit Crumble

(v 4)
CALORIES: 199

Any combination of dried fruits can be used for this dish – experiment to find the flavour you like the best.

PREPARATION TIME: 15 MINUTES
COOKING TIME: 45 MINUTES

TEMPERATURE: 190°C/375°F/GAS 5

INGREDIENTS: IMPERIAL/METRIC
4oz/125g dried prunes, stoned
2oz/50g currants
2oz/50g raisins
2oz/50g dried dates
½pt/250ml unsweetened pineapple juice
1 fresh banana
1tsp ground cinnamon
1tsp mixed spice
8oz/225g oats
2tbsp honey

METHOD
1   Wash the dried fruit well.
2   Soak overnight in the fruit juice.
3   Place all the ingredients, except the oats and honey, in a saucepan and add the juice.
4   Bring to the boil and simmer for about 20 minutes – until the fruit is soft and the liquid has thickened.
5   Heat the honey and mix with the oats. Place the fruit in an ovenproof dish and pile on the topping. Bake until brown and crispy, about 25 minutes.
6   Serve either hot or cold with natural unsweetened yogurt.

TIP BOX

Dates have been cultivated for over 5,000 years in the Middle East and are well known as a sugar substitute – both for wine and food. They are also a good source of nutrients and fibre.

Strawberry Cheesecake

(v 6)

PREPARATION TIME: 20 MINUTES
CHILLING TIME: 3 HOURS

INGREDIENTS: IMPERIAL/METRIC

Traditional Recipe
CALORIES: 575

8oz/225g digestive biscuits, crushed
3oz/75g butter, melted
6oz/175g double cream
8oz/225g full-fat soft cheese
8oz/225g strawberries, halved

Swap Shop Recipe
CALORIES: 233

8oz/225g rolled oats
1 orange, zest of
3tbsp clear honey
6oz/175g quark (low-fat cheese)
8oz/225g low-fat set natural yogurt
8oz/225g strawberries, halved

METHOD

1 Mix together the rolled oats, orange zest and 2tbsp of the honey. Press firmly into an 8in/20cm flan case.
2 Mix the quark with the yogurt and the remaining honey.
3 Spoon into the flan case and arrange the fruit on top.
4 Chill for 3 hours.

TIP BOX

Fruits with tough skins and pips contain more fibre
than fleshy soft fruits.

Pineapple Cheesecake

(F V 4)
CALORIES: 273

You can ring the changes with this recipe by making the
base from bran and honey. It is also an excellent dessert
for a formal dinner party.

PREPARATION TIME: 45 MINUTES
COOKING TIME: 35 MINUTES
TEMPERATURE: 170°C/340°F/GAS 3

INGREDIENTS: IMPERIAL/METRIC
2oz/50g polyunsaturated margarine (unhydrogenated)
8oz/225g medium oats, toasted
3tbsp honey
12oz/350g low-fat vegetarian soft cheese
½oz/15g wholemeal flour
1 lemon, zest and juice
1oz/25g sunflower seeds, ground
3 egg whites
1lb/450g pineapple, peeled and chopped into segments

METHOD
1   Make the base by melting the margarine and mixing
    with the oats and 1tbsp of the honey. Pack this

    mixture hard into the base of a loose-sided 8in/20cm flan or cake tin.

2   Beat the cheese until softened.

3   Add the flour, lemon juice, zest, remaining honey and ground seeds.

4   Beat the egg whites until stiff and carefully fold into the mixture.

5   Spread this carefully over the oat base and level.

6   Arrange pineapple segments attractively on top of the mixture.

7   Bake until heated through and just beginning to turn a very pale golden brown, about 35 minutes.

8   Cover with foil towards the end of the cooking period if it looks like being too brown.

9   Leave to cool completely on a wire tray before removing from the tin.

TIP BOX

Yellow melons, peaches and apricots are the best
source of vitamin A in fruit.

Plum Crunch

(F V 8)
CALORIES: 195

This was invented for my dad who loves plums in tarts and crumbles but has always eaten them made with lots of white sugar and white flour. This tastes better and is far healthier.

PREPARATION TIME: 30 MINUTES
COOKING TIME: 40 MINUTES
TEMPERATURE: 160°C/325°F/GAS 3

INGREDIENTS: IMPERIAL/METRIC
1lb/450g eating plums, washed, stoned and halved
4tbsp honey
2oz/50g polyunsaturated margarine (unhydrogenated)
4oz/125g wholemeal flour
2oz/50g barley flakes
1oz/25g jumbo oats
2tbsp sunflower seeds
2tbsp sesame oil

METHOD
1   Place the plums in a large, shallow, ovenproof dish.
2   Warm the honey and pour 2tbsp over the plums.
3   Rub the margarine into the flour until the mixture resembles fine breadcrumbs.
4   Add the barley flakes, jumbo oats and seeds.
5   Add the rest of the warm honey and stir into the mixture.
6   Add the oil and mix well.
7   Place on top of the plum mixture and bake until the topping is golden brown and crisp, about 40 minutes.

Prune and Banana Yogurt

(v 4)
CALORIES: 78

A lovely rich creamy dessert that is quick to make and very healthy!

PREPARATION TIME: 10 MINUTES
CHILLING TIME: OVERNIGHT

INGREDIENTS: IMPERIAL/METRIC
4oz/125g prunes, washed, pitted and chopped
1 banana, sliced
½pt/250ml natural unsweetened low-fat yogurt

METHOD
1 Mix the prunes and banana with the yogurt.
2 Pile the mixture into a serving dish and leave in the refrigerator overnight to thicken.
3 Serve chilled.

TIP BOX

Fresh fruits consist of 80–90 per cent water.

CHAPTER TWELVE

YOU CAN HAVE YOUR CAKE AND EAT IT!

YOU MAY be asking yourself how a chapter on cakes, of all things, finds its way into a book concerned solely with healthy eating. Cakes are a treat, naughty but nice, in which to indulge from time to time. And then, perhaps, you feel guilty afterwards, for surely all the sugar, butter, white flour and eggs that form the basis of a cake must be bad for the health? Well, yes, these ingredients are bad for our health in one way or another, but almost everything in a cake that is unhealthy can be replaced by something that is better for our health.

Eating a healthy diet definitely does not mean that you have to abstain from enjoying cakes. And I do mean ENJOY. Many people believe that a healthier type of cake, by its very nature, must be so heavy that it sinks to the base of your stomach like lead. It is regarded as something to be endured and certainly not enjoyed. Richard and I have encountered such cakes in many a healthfood restaurant and in my opinion they should sport a government health warning. But they don't have to be like that.

I enjoy a nice piece of cake with a cup of tea – and Richard certainly does – so over the years I have developed a whole range of cakes which are not only delicious but healthy as well. Most of them can also double up as puddings – especially if you warm the slices up in a microwave or gently steam them over a pan of boiling water for a few minutes. This transforms the cakes into light, fluffy desserts which taste wonderful with some concentrated soya milk poured over them.

Quite often I experiment by using vegetables as the base for a cake recipe. Would you believe that you can make a cake with grated courgettes? Such a cake was among the food that I had taken along to a Miriam Stoppard show in which I was appearing and the film crew absolutely loved it. They could not believe that it was an example of a healthy cake – it tasted too good! So don't be deterred, you really can have your cake and eat it!

COMMON PROBLEMS

There are two main problems which people seem to experience when making a 'healthy' cake: the cake is either too dry or too heavy.

I am often asked why a 'healthy' cake turns out extremely dry and crumbly. There is nothing as discouraging as slicing a cake and watching each slice disintegrate into a pile of crumbs. Nor is it very impressive.

The cause is simple, and easy to remedy. If you use wholemeal flour instead of white you should add a little extra liquid to the mixture because wholemeal flours are more dense and so absorb more liquid. There is no strict rule as to how much extra liquid is needed as each type of flour will vary. Even different batches of the same flour will vary in absorbency. However, a good yardstick is to check the consistency of the mixture, which should be firm enough to stick to a tablespoon and yet runny enough to drop off the spoon fairly easily. Remember that when you substitute honey, or a dried date purée, for sugar you are also adding extra liquid. You will adapt very quickly to this new method of cake making until, before you know it, you do it without even thinking.

A cake that is too heavy can be quite unpalatable and, once again, it seems to be synonymous with a 'healthy' cake. Again the main culprit is the wholemeal flour. The bran and husk of the grain are retained in wholemeal flour which makes it heavier than the white processed type. Cakes do, therefore, have a tendency to be heavier if made with wholemeal flour.

There are steps you can take to remedy this problem. Try mixing the wholemeal flour with other types, such as barley flour, brown rice flour or even white flour, as this will help lighten the cake. Many people will no doubt complain if I advocate the use of white flour. I justify its use because people can become so discouraged with trying to eat a healthy diet that they abandon the attempt completely. This defeats the object and so I see little wrong in a compromise. The idea is to improve your diet. In my opinion it is far better to use 50 per cent white flour than to revert to 100 per cent.

You can also lighten a cake by adding one or two teaspoons of low-sodium baking powder to the flour or by using 85 per cent, rather than 100 per cent wholemeal flour. The 100 per cent variety is heavier because it contains all the bran, germ and husk of the wheat grain, whereas the other variety contains only 85 per cent. It is surprising what a difference the use of this lighter flour makes to the cake.

Healthy eating should be enjoyable, not something to put up with for the sake of your health, and cakes are no exception.

SWAP SHOP RECIPES

No doubt you will have made cakes that have become firm favourites with your family and, understandably, you will feel a little reluctant to toss them to one side. Well, it is often quite easy to make that old familiar cake much more healthy by simply making one or two changes to the ingredients. And once you are familiar with the process, it will become second nature.

To give you an idea of exactly what I mean I have converted traditional cake recipes, which are probably familiar to you, into much healthier versions of the same thing. Using this technique you will be able to convert any recipe you wish. But remember, there are no hard and fast rules about the conversion process and it does tend to come down to trial and error in the end. However, using my swap shop recipes as a guide should help you to master the technique.

Marrow and Orange Cake

(F V 8)
CALORIES: 243

Everyone thought I had gone too far with this one – until they tasted it!

PREPARATION TIME: 25 MINUTES
COOKING TIME: 65 MINUTES
TEMPERATURE: 180°C/350°F/GAS 4

INGREDIENTS: IMPERIAL/METRIC
6oz/175g marrow, peeled, seeded and cut
into small cubes
4oz/100g polyunsaturated margarine (unhydrogenated)
3oz/75g honey
2 egg whites
1 orange, zest and juice
10oz/275g wholemeal flour
4tsp low-sodium baking powder
1 orange, peeled and sliced

METHOD
1   Oil and line an 8in/20cm cake tin.
2   Steam marrow for 10 minutes. Leave to cool.
3   Beat together the margarine and honey until thoroughly mixed.
4   Add egg white gradually, beating well.
5   Add orange zest, juice and marrow. Stir well.
6   Sift the flour and baking powder into the mixture. Stir well.
7   Spoon the mixture into the prepared tin.
8   Arrange the orange slices on top of the cake.
9   Bake until well risen and golden brown, about 1 hour. Turn out and cool on a wire rack.

Chocolate Cake

(F V 8)

PREPARATION TIME: 20 MINUTES
COOKING TIME: 30 MINUTES
TEMPERATURE: 180°C/350°F/GAS 4

INGREDIENTS: IMPERIAL/METRIC

Traditional Recipe
CALORIES: 493

8oz/225g self-raising flour
2tbsp cocoa powder
6oz/175g sugar
4oz/125g butter
8fl oz/225ml water
2 eggs, beaten

TOPPING/FILLING
½pt/250ml double cream, whipped
2oz/50g chocolate, melted

Swap Shop Recipe
CALORIES: 227

8oz/225g wholemeal flour
3tsp low-sodium baking powder
2oz/50g sugar
6tbsp polyunsaturated oil
8fl oz/225ml water
2 egg whites, beaten
2 tbsp carob powder

TOPPING/FILLING
½pt/250ml fromage frais
2oz/50g carob 'chocolate' bar, melted

METHOD

1   Lightly oil and base-line two 7in/18cm sandwich tins.

2   Sift the flour, baking powder and carob powder into a bowl. Add the sugar and stir in the oil, water and egg whites. Mix until smooth.

3   Pour into the two tins and bake until the centre of the cakes springs back to a light touch, about 30 minutes. Turn on to a wire rack to cook. Remove the paper.

4   Carefully fold the melted carob into the fromage frais and use to sandwich the two cakes together and for decoration.

Pineapple Fruit Cake

(F V 8)
CALORIES: 309

An unusual combination of dried and fresh fruit that tastes refreshingly different. The cake is nice and moist and cuts well. It also keeps very well, provided you wrap it carefully in greaseproof paper and foil.

PREPARATION TIME: 35 MINUTES
COOKING TIME: 75 MINUTES
TEMPERATURE: 160°C/325°F/GAS 3

INGREDIENTS: IMPERIAL/METRIC
6oz/175g dried dates, washed and pitted
4oz/100g raisins, washed
4oz/100g currants, washed
4oz/100g pineapple, fresh if possible otherwise use tinned without added sugar, but drain well

4oz/100g grated carrot
7oz/200g wholemeal flour
3tsp low-sodium baking powder
2 lemons, zest of
7tbsp pineapple juice, unsweetened

TOPPING
2tbsp pineapple juice, unsweetened
½tsp Gelozone
1oz/25g pineapple, chopped

METHOD
1   Grease an 8in/20cm round cake tin.
2   Place the dates in a small saucepan with just enough boiling water to cover. Bring to the boil and simmer for about 10 minutes until soft and pulpy. Leave to cool slightly.
3   Mix together the remaining dried fruit, pineapple, carrot, flour, baking powder and lemon zest.
4   Add the juice and date mixture.
5   Spoon into the prepared tin and bake until firm to the touch, about 1 hour and 15 minutes.
6   To make the topping: gently heat the pineapple juice. Sprinkle on the Gelozone and whisk vigorously. Do not allow to boil. Once the juice begins to steam it will be ready. Add the pineapple chunks and spread the mixture over the fruit cake while it is still warm.

TIP BOX
I find that the quickest way to remove the zest from an orange or lemon is with a utensil called a 'zester'. It not only saves time and effort but looks more attractive as well. Always scrub the fruit well first.

Passion Cake
(F V 8)

PREPARATION TIME: 25 MINUTES
COOKING TIME: 40 MINUTES
TEMPERATURE: 190°C/375°F/GAS 5

INGREDIENTS: IMPERIAL/METRIC

Traditional Recipe
CALORIES: 454

4oz/100g butter
6oz/175g sugar
½tsp nutmeg
1 lemon, zest of
3 eggs, beaten
5oz/150g self-raising flour
3oz/75g grated carrot
2oz/50g cashew nuts

FILLING
8oz/225g full-fat cream cheese
3oz/75g cashew nuts, crushed
2oz/50g sugar

Swap Shop Recipe
CALORIES: 251

4oz/100g polyunsaturated margarine (unhydrogenated)
3oz/75g muscovado sugar
1tsp ground cinnamon
½tsp grated nutmeg
1 lemon, zest of
2 eggs, beaten
5oz/150g wholemeal flour, plain
3tsp low-sodium baking powder
3oz/75g grated carrot
1oz/25g walnut halves

FILLING
8oz/225g low-fat soft cheese
3oz/75g walnuts, crushed
½ mango, chopped finely

METHOD
1   Lightly oil two 7in/18cm sandwich tins.
2   Beat together the margarine and sugar until the mixture is light and fluffy. Beat in the cinnamon, nutmeg and lemon zest.
3   Add the eggs gradually, beating well with each addition.
4   Sift together the flour and baking powder and fold gently into the egg mixture.
5   Fold in the grated carrot, walnuts and 1tbsp of warm water.
6   Divide the mixture between the tins and bake until the sides of the cake just come away from the tins a little. Turn out on to a wire rack to cool.
7   Beat the cheese until soft and creamy and fold in the nuts and chopped mango. Spread this mixture between the two cakes and sandwich together.

Sticky Prune and Date Cake

(F V 8)
CALORIES: 296

If, like me, you enjoy sticky, substantial cakes, then you will love this recipe. It is particularly good served with natural low-fat yogurt. The prunes give the cake a laxative effect because they contain a natural substance similar to biscodyl – the active ingredient in many laxatives and suppositories!

PREPARATION TIME: 35 MINUTES
COOKING TIME: 45 MINUTES
TEMPERATURE: 180°C/350°F/GAS 4

INGREDIENTS: IMPERIAL/METRIC
4oz/125g dried dates, washed and pitted
4oz/125g dried prunes, washed and pitted
4fl oz/125ml sesame seed oil (cold pressed)
1 egg white
1tbsp tahini
5oz/150g wholemeal flour
2tsp low-sodium baking powder
½tsp freshly grated nutmeg
1tsp ground cinnamon
3fl oz/75ml soya milk

TOPPING
2tbsp soya milk
1tbsp honey
1tbsp blackstrap molasses
few drops natural vanilla essence

METHOD

1 Oil and line an 8in/20cm round cake tin.
2 Place the dates in a saucepan and just cover with water. Bring to the boil and simmer until soft and pulpy. Do the same in another saucepan with the prunes. Leave both to cool slightly.
3 Drain the prunes and chop roughly.
4 In a bowl whisk together the dates, oil, egg white and tahini until the mixture is thick and fluffy.
5 Sift the flour, baking powder and spices. Stir into the date mixture.
6 Add the prunes and milk.
7 Pour mixture into the tin and bake for 45 minutes or until firm to the touch.
8 Warm all the topping ingredients together in a pan.
9 Once the cake is removed from the oven prick the top all over with a skewer and pour the warm topping over it.
10 Leave to cool in the tin. This is also nice served as a hot pudding with soya concentrated milk.

TIP BOX

A cake cooked in a microwave looks completely different to one cooked conventionally. The texture is softer and is more reminiscent of a steamed pudding than a cake. But be careful not to overcook in the microwave or you could wind up with a cinder. I speak from experience! As soon as the cake begins to shrink away from the sides of the mould it should be ready.

CHAPTER THIRTEEN

ANYONE FOR AFTERNOON TEA?

THE ENGLISH tradition of afternoon tea has declined over the years as the pace of life quickens. But it is still nice (and good for you!) once in a while to relax for a few precious minutes with a cup of tea and a home-made treat.

The scones are particularly adaptable: try adding different dried fruits and fruit zests. And don't stop at sweet variations, try herbs and spices as well. Herb scones are nice served with soups and salads.

COMMON PROBLEMS

Why do wholemeal scones always crumble? Well, the answer is they don't have to. The problem arises because of the nature of wholemeal flour. White flour is much lighter than wholemeal because it has had all the bran and husk removed and, therefore, is less absorbent. The secret of non-crumbly scones is to add more liquid to the mixture when using wholemeal flour. The dough should be firm, soft, pliable and should not crumble when you are rolling it out. When using a purée of dried dates to sweeten the scones you will automatically be using more liquid, so you must take this into account.

I like my scones to be heavy and substantial, but Richard doesn't. A reasonable compromise is to use three quarters wholemeal flour and a quarter white flour – you could even use half and half, or, as suggested in Chapter 12, use 85 per cent wholemeal flour.

SWAP SHOP RECIPES

Converting scone and biscuit recipes is quite straight-forward and most require only minimal changes. The main changes will be in the dairy products and the type of flour you use.

Fruit and Nut Scones

(F V 15)

PREPARATION TIME: 15 MINUTES
COOKING TIME: 15–20 MINUTES
TEMPERATURE: 190°C/375°F/GAS 5

INGREDIENTS: IMPERIAL/METRIC

Traditional Recipe
CALORIES: 152

8oz/225g self-raising flour
2oz/50g butter
4oz/125g sugar
2oz/50g peanuts
1 egg, beaten
2tbsp cream
4tbsp milk
2tbsp cashew nuts, crushed

Swap Shop Recipe
CALORIES: 101

4oz/115g plain flour, white
4oz/115g wholemeal flour
3tsp low-sodium baking powder
2oz/50g polyunsaturated margarine (unhydrogenated)
2oz/50g dried apricots, washed and chopped
2oz/50g walnuts, crushed
1 egg, beaten
2tbsp Greek strained yogurt
4tbsp skimmed milk
2tbsp cracked wheat (burghul)

METHOD

1 Sift the flours and baking powder into a bowl and rub in the margarine until the mixture looks like breadcrumbs. Mix in the apricots and walnuts.

2 Mix the egg with the yogurt and 3tbsp of the milk. Add to the dry ingredients and mix to a fairly soft dough.

3 Roll out the dough to about ¾in/2cm thick and stamp out ten 2in/5cm rounds with a cutter.

4 Place on a lightly oiled baking tray. Lightly brush the tops with the remaining milk and sprinkle on the cracked wheat.

5 Bake until golden brown, 15–20 minutes.

Apple Scone Ring
(F V 8)
CALORIES: 160

This is lovely toasted and eaten warm. I prefer the chopped apples to be quite 'chunky' as this gives a nice texture and you retain the distinctive flavours of the scone. You can, if you prefer, grate the apples and this will give a smoother scone with an even flavour throughout.

PREPARATION TIME: 15 MINUTES
COOKING TIME: 25 MINUTES
TEMPERATURE: 200°C/400F/GAS 6

INGREDIENTS: IMPERIAL/METRIC
1 cooking apple, large
8oz/225g wholemeal flour
3tsp low-sodium baking powder
2oz/50g polyunsaturated margarine (unhydrogenated)
1oz/25g honey
3fl /oz/75ml soya milk (sugar free)
2tsp raw brown sugar

METHOD
1 Peel, core and finely chop the apple.
2 Sift together the flour and baking powder.
3 Rub in the margarine.
4 Add the honey and chopped apple.
5 Add enough milk to form a soft dough.
6 On a lightly floured surface form into a large round ½in/1cm thick and place on a greased baking tray.
7 Brush the top with a little milk and sprinkle with the raw brown sugar.
8 Bake until risen and golden brown, about 25 minutes.

Fruit Scones

(F V 8)
CALORIES: 266

Try lemon and grapefruit as a change from the orange flavouring.

PREPARATION TIME: 15 MINUTES
COOKING TIME: 15–20 MINUTES
TEMPERATURE: 220°C/420°F/GAS 7

INGREDIENTS: IMPERIAL/METRIC
8oz/225g wholemeal flour
2tsp low-sodium baking powder
3oz/75g polyunsaturated margarine (unhydrogenated)
1 orange, zest and juice
3oz/75g raisins
½oz/15g molasses
4fl oz/125ml soya milk

METHOD

1 Sieve the flour and baking powder into a bowl and rub in the margarine until the mixture resembles fine breadcrumbs.
2 Stir in the orange zest, juice, raisins, molasses and enough milk to make a fairly soft dough.
3 Knead the mixture gently on a lightly floured surface.
4 Roll out to a thickness of 1in/2.5cm and cut into rounds with a cutter.
5 Place on a greased baking sheet and bake for 15–20 minutes, until well risen and golden brown. Cool on a wire tray.

Crunch Bites

(F V 8)
CALORIES: 233

Biscuits which are home-made bear no resemblance at all to shop-bought versions. I like my biscuits to be crunchy and substantial – this recipe fits the bill very nicely.

PREPARATION TIME: 20 MINUTES
COOKING TIME: 15 MINUTES
TEMPERATURE: 180°C/350°F/GAS 4

INGREDIENTS: IMPERIAL/METRIC
2oz/50g dried dates, washed and pitted
4oz/100g polyunsaturated margarine (unhydrogenated)
2oz/50g honey
6oz/175g wholemeal flour, self-raising
1oz/25g jumbo oats
1oz/25g barley flakes
1oz/25g prunes, chopped
2oz/50g sunflower seeds
1tsp mixed spice, ground
1 orange, zest of
1 lemon, zest of
2tsp low-sodium baking powder

METHOD
1   Place the dates in a small saucepan with enough boiling water just to cover them. Simmer for 15 minutes until the dates are soft and pulpy. Leave to cool.
2   Melt the margarine.
3   Remove from the heat and stir in all the remaining ingredients.

4 Press the mixture into eight evenly sized balls.
5 Place well apart on a greased baking sheet and flatten slightly.
6 Bake for about 15 minutes until risen and golden brown.
7 Cool on a wire tray.

TIP BOX

Always use plain flour and add your own low-sodium baking powder. This way you minimize the offending sodium.

Orange and Ginger Shortbread

(F V 8)

PREPARATION TIME: 10 MINUTES
COOKING TIME: 40 MINUTES
TEMPERATURE: 150°C/300°F/GAS 2

INGREDIENTS: IMPERIAL/METRIC

Traditional Recipe
CALORIES: 216

4oz/100g butter
6oz/175g plain flour
1tsp ground ginger
4oz/100g sugar
1 orange, zest of

Swap Shop Recipe
CALORIES: 185

4oz/100g polyunsaturated margarine (unhydrogenated)
6oz/175g wholemeal flour, plain
1tsp ground ginger
2oz/50g muscovado sugar
1 orange, zest of

METHOD

1 Rub the margarine into the flour until the mixture resembles fine breadcrumbs.
2 Stir in the ginger, sugar and orange zest and knead to a firm dough.
3 Turn out on to a lightly floured surface and divide into two.
4 Roll each half into a 7in/18cm round and place on a baking sheet. Mark each round into eight portions and prick all over with a fork.
5 Bake until light golden brown, about 40 minutes. Leave to cool on the baking tray.

TIP BOX

If you are short of time and fancy home-baked biscuits, mix a little honey into some muesli, put teaspoonfuls of this mixture on a lightly greased baking sheet and bake at 180°C/350°F/Gas 4.

Hot Poppyseed Rolls

(F V 8)

CALORIES: 155

This must be my most 'asked for' recipe. These little round balls are full of flavour and look very attractive. They have a 'nutty', crunchy texture and are nice fresh from the oven, with a little 'healthy' margarine and low-fat soft cheese.

PREPARATION TIME: 10 MINUTES
COOKING TIME: 20 MINUTES
TEMPERATURE: 230°C/450°F/GAS 8

INGREDIENTS: IMPERIAL/METRIC
8oz/225g wholemeal flour
3tsp low-sodium baking powder
¼tsp low-sodium salt
2oz/50g polyunsaturated margarine (unhydrogenated)
2tbsp sunflower seeds, roasted
1tbsp poppy seeds
6tbsp soya milk

METHOD

1 Sift the flour, baking powder and salt into a bowl and rub in the margarine.
2 Add the seeds and mix well.
3 Mix in enough milk to give a soft dough.
4 Form into eight evenly sized balls and place on a greased baking sheet.
5 Brush the tops with soya milk.
6 Bake until well risen and golden brown, about 20 minutes.
7 Serve hot with soup or pâté.

INDEX

All Pan books are available at your local bookshop or newsagent, or can be ordered direct from the publisher. Indicate the number of copies required and fill in the form below.

Send to: **CS Department, Pan Books Ltd., P.O. Box 40,
             Basingstoke, Hants.   RG21 2YT.**

or phone: 0256 469551 (Ansaphone), quoting title, author
             and Credit Card number.

Please enclose a remittance* to the value of the cover price plus: 60p for the first book plus 30p per copy for each additional book ordered to a maximum charge of £2.40 to cover postage and packing.

*Payment may be made in sterling by UK personal cheque, postal order, sterling draft or international money order, made payable to Pan Books Ltd.

Alternatively by Barclaycard/Access:

Card No. ⬚⬚⬚⬚⬚⬚⬚⬚⬚⬚⬚⬚⬚⬚⬚⬚

Signature:

Applicable only in the UK and Republic of Ireland.

While every effort is made to keep prices low, it is sometimes necessary to increase prices at short notice. Pan Books reserve the right to show on covers and charge new retail prices which may differ from those advertised in the text or elsewhere.

NAME AND ADDRESS IN BLOCK LETTERS PLEASE:

....

Name ————————————————————————————

Address ——————————————————————————

————————————————————————————————

————————————————————————————————

————————————————————————————————